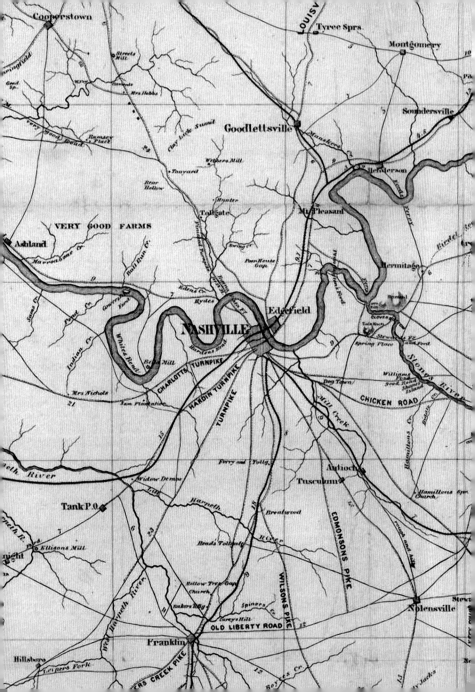

NASHVILLE
COCKTAILS

AN ELEGANT COLLECTION
OF OVER 100 RECIPES
INSPIRED BY MUSIC CITY

DELIA JO RAMSEY

CIDER MILL
PRESS

BOOK
PUBLISHERS

NASHVILLE COCKTAILS

ISBN-13: 978-1-40034-066-8
ISBN-10: 1-40034-066-7

This book may be ordered by mail from the publisher. Please include $5.99 for postage and handling. Please support your local bookseller first!

Books published by Cider Mill Press Book Publishers are available at special discounts for bulk purchases in the United States by corporations, institutions, and other organizations. For more information, please contact the publisher.

Cider Mill Press Book Publishers
"Where good books are ready for press"
501 Nelson Place
Nashville, Tennessee 37214
cidermillpress.com

Typography: Rosewood Std, Avenir, Copperplate, Sackers, Warnock

Photography credits on page 324

Printed in India

24 25 26 27 28 REP 5 4 3 2 1

First Edition

CONTENTS

INTRODUCTION

Welcome to Music City, USA, where the cocktail scene is as hot as the humid summers and the country music. Jokingly known by locals as "a drinking town with a music problem," Nashville, called out in dozens of drinking songs, attracts millions of visitors every year who are looking for a good time. But while Nashville is well known for its country music shows at the Ryman Auditorium; its Titans, Predators, and Nashville SC games; its bachelorette parties, or for tourists trying to catch a glimpse of a country music superstar in the wild, there's a lot more to Tennessee's capital city than these.

MODERN NASHVILLE AT A GLANCE

For one, Nashville has finally arrived as a worldwide cocktail destination. Noteworthy cocktail bars born in New York and other world cities have opened Nashville outposts over the last few years, with Attaboy and Liquor Lab elevating the experience of ordering a drink during a night out on the town.

While the masses clog up Lower Broadway to booze it up, the heart of real cocktail culture in Music City lies in its neighborhoods surrounding the city center. Locals and serious cocktail enthusiasts alike flock to East Nashville, Germantown, Wedgewood-Houston, Midtown, and other sections of Downtown to sip libations crafted with Tennessee whiskey, real-deal moonshine, and more. If you're looking for the origin story of Nashville nightlife, pop over to Printers Alley, which was known for decades as a "sinful" street, where the story goes that secret passageways helped Al Capone and his organization and others smuggle booze up from the Cumberland River.

One longtime Nashville drinking tradition that has carried into today is the iconic "holler and swaller," a cheerful Music City toast that literally means to shout and drink. You're guaranteed a good time if you hear a band making this toast at a Nashville honky-tonk.

TENNESSEE TEETOTALERS AND NASHVILLE'S DRY PAST

Nashville being the party town it is today, it's hard to believe that, just over fifty years ago, you couldn't even order a drink at a bar in Davidson County. In fact, Tennessee has had quite the rocky relationship with alcohol through the years. Some of the first temperance societies on record were born in Tennessee. As early as 1829, societies were organized in both Nashville and Kingsport, with plenty of local press in Maryville, Tullahoma, and Nashville supporting their teetotaling cause. Joining the temperance movement were the Women's Christian Temperance Union (WCTU) and Anti-Saloon League.

Nine years later, in 1838, the state's legislature was the very first in the young United States to pass a law of prohibition against alcohol. This law stated that you could not sell hard liquor in taverns or in stores. Breaking this law was ruled as a misdemeanor, which was not exactly enough to stop the flow of alcohol across Tennessee.

It's a good time to mention the origin story of a certain world-famous whiskey distillery with roots in Lynchburg, just about ninety minutes southeast of downtown Nashville. Jasper "Jack" Daniel regis-

The Tennessee Capitol (background) and train depot (foreground), 1864

tered his distillery in 1866, and today Jack Daniel's Distillery stands as the oldest registered distillery in the United States.

Fast-forward to 1909. Tennessee's state senate passed two prohibition-related bills, one outlawing the sale or consumption of booze within four miles of a public or private school, the second banning the manufacture of all alcoholic beverages within the state. Governor Malcolm R. Patterson vetoed both bills but was subsequently overridden by the General Assembly.

The campaign against alcohol continued. In 1917, Governor Thomas C. Rye's "bone-dry bill" passed, outlawing the receipt or possession of liquor and prohibiting the transportation of liquor into or out of the state. The federal government caught up with Tennessee in 1919 with the passage of the 18th Amendment. Federal Prohibition banned the production, sale, and transport of alcohol nationwide. For fourteen years, Prohibition was the law of the land. It wasn't until 1933 that the 21st Amendment officially repealed the 18th Amendment and ended nationwide Prohibition—the only amendment to nullify another amendment in American history.

But that didn't stop the temperance movement in the South. As recently as the late 1960s, Nashville was still semi-dry. Stories go that the answer to this was just to know the right people, and to BYO bottle, but to bring it back home at the end of the night. It is said that police would look the other way, and restaurants would allow patrons to store their liquor labeled behind the bar, or would just sell it to them in spite of the laws.

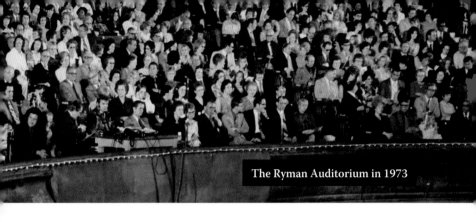

MUSIC AND BOOZE GO HAND IN HAND IN MUSIC CITY

Whether legal or not, alcohol has always been part of the story in Nashville. The lyrics of thousands of songs reflect the drinking culture of Music City, and even the bluegrass standard, "Rocky Top," gives a nod to the state's rebellious moonshining past.

Supposedly, husband-and-wife songwriting duo Felice and Boudleaux Bryant wrote "Rocky Top" in just ten minutes, back in 1967. The song became Tennessee's official state song in 1982 and also serves as the University of Tennessee's fight song.

Once two strangers climbed ol' Rocky Top,
lookin' for a moonshine still.
Strangers ain't come down from Rocky Top;
reckon they never will.
Corn won't grow at all on Rocky Top;
dirt's too rocky by far.
That's why all the folks on Rocky Top
get their corn from a jar.

WHITE LIGHTNING

Production of moonshine, the notoriously incendiary "rebel spirit" of the South, dates back to the late 1700s, when Scottish and Irish immigrants settled into southern Appalachia. They brought with them their distilling practices from the Old World, as well as their recipes for what is typically a white whiskey derived from corn, yeast, sugar, and water. Until recent years, this kind of distilling was illegal. Known also as "skullpop," "hooch," "white lightning," "wildcat," and a host of other monikers, moonshine originally got its name from its being made beneath the light of the moon to evade law enforcement. Even post-Prohibition, moonshining continued in the South—especially in dry counties. It wasn't until 2010 that the state legalized the production, distillation, and sale of the region's infamous spirit. That's when Tennessee's first legal moonshine distillery, Ole Smoky Distillery, was born.

NASHVILLE TIPS

If you order an alcoholic beverage in Nashville, be aware that the liquor-by-the-drink tax rate is 15 percent. With a few exceptions, wine and high-ABV beer (9% or more) sold for consumption on premises is eligible for the "sin tax."

If you're visiting Nashville, be sure that you venture beyond the basics. While it's nice to sip bourbon inside a music-filled Lower Broadway honky-tonk, also check out a local dive bar for a beer and a shot, sip gimlets on Gallatin, or grab a Mule a stone's throw from Music Row. And if you're not drinking, don't fret—the city's alcohol-free scene is having a moment, too, with zero-proof bottle shops, liquor-free pop-ups, exciting boozeless pairings, and thoughtfully crafted drinks making hangover-free waves across the city.

Cheers, y'all!

BASIC COCKTAIL TECHNIQUES AND PREPARATIONS TO KNOW

DRY-SHAKE

When a recipe asks you to "dry-shake," that means to combine all of the drink's ingredients in a cocktail shaker tin—without ice—and shake. The dry shake is often used to emulsify drinks that include an egg white.

WET-SHAKE

The reason it's called the "wet shake" is because of the condensation that forms on the outside of the cocktail shaker during shaking. When a recipe asks you to "wet-shake," that means to vigorously shake a cocktail shaker filled with ice in addition to the cocktail ingredients to create a more diluted and chilled drink.

WHIP-SHAKE

This involves rapidly shaking a cocktail shaker or mixing tin back and forth with both hands while keeping a tight grip on it, using a minimal amount of ice. This creates a frothy texture and adds considerably more air bubbles to the drink.

DOUBLE-STRAIN

What about those pesky ice shards that end up in your drink? That's where the double strain comes in. That involves straining the drink twice—once through a regular strainer (i.e., a Hawthorne strainer) and then again through a fine-mesh strainer. This ensures that any ice shards or small pieces of fruit, herbs, or spices are caught and do not end up in the final cocktail.

SIMPLE SYRUP (1:1)

In a saucepan, combine equal parts sugar and water. (Most people use white granulated sugar, but feel free to experiment with other types like brown or raw sugar.) Bring the mixture to a simmer over medium heat, stirring it until the sugar fully dissolves. Once the sugar is dissolved, remove the pan from heat and let it cool. After it has cooled, you can pour your simple syrup into a clean glass jar or bottle, and store it in the refrigerator and use it within 1 or 2 weeks.

SUGARED RIM

Fill a small bowl with ¼ cup water and another small bowl with ¼ cup granulated sugar. Dip the rim of the glass in the bowl filled with water, then roll the rim of the glass in the sugar, ensuring an even coating. Then, gently shake off any excess sugar.

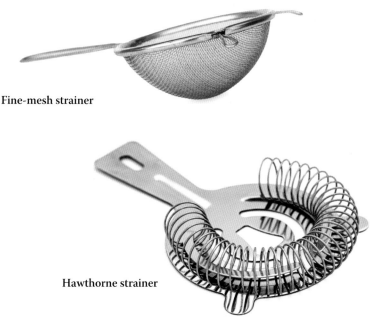

Fine-mesh strainer

Hawthorne strainer

TOOLS TO BUILD YOUR NASHVILLE BAR AT HOME

GLASSWARE

Coupe glass
Rocks glass
Collins glass
Cocktail glass
Double rocks glass

Hurricane glass
Tiki mug
Glencairn whiskey glass
Small brandy snifter

TOOLS

Cocktail shaker
Mixing glass
Strainers (conical, Hawthorne, julep)
Stainless-steel / Japanese-style jigger
Peeler, Y-peeler
Large ice cube molds (for large rocks and spheres)

Muddler
Barspoon (teardrop end)
Basic measuring tool
Channel knife
Immersion blender
Cocktail picks
Handheld citrus juicer
Punch bowl

Coupe glass

Hurricane glass

TENNESSEE WHISKEY SHOPPING LIST

Nelson's Green Brier Tennessee Whiskey
Uncle Nearest 1856 Premium Aged Whiskey
George Dickel Classic Recipe
Jack Daniel's Bonded Tennessee Whiskey
Jack Daniel's Old No. 7
Chattanooga Whiskey 91

Immersion blender

Rocks glass

Collins glass

Barspoon

NASHVILLE TOP 5: BLAKE ELLS, MUSIC JOURNALIST

Blake Ells is the associate editor of *Country Insider* and has appeared in *Rolling Stone, No Depression, Taste of Country, The Boot*, AL.com, and more. He is the author of *The Muscle Shoals Legacy of FAME* and *Magic City Rock: Spaces and Faces of Birmingham's Scene*, available from The History Press. Raised in Rogersville, Alabama, a one-and-a-half stoplight town, Blake now lives in Nashville. Here, he shares some of his top places to grab a drink and catch some live music. Plus, he gives us a playlist—all by Nashville natives you might not have realized were "Nashville unicorns."

AMERICAN LEGION POST 82 (INGLEWOOD: EAST NASHVILLE)

One of Nashville's finest honky-tonks is also a gathering spot for local veterans, but the good news is that it's open to anyone. Each week, the post hosts Honky Tonk Tuesdays, which kick off with dance lessons at 7 p.m. The post also features Bluegrass Wednesdays and offers songwriting workshops for veterans. The music swings and the beer is cold.

DEE'S COUNTRY COCKTAIL LOUNGE (MADISON)

The de facto home of Nashville's Americana community. You'll regularly find Jon Byrd or Jon Latham on stage, and you may find yourself sitting beside any number of artists—it's your favorite artist's favorite bar. Try the frito pie.

ROBERT'S WESTERN WORLD (LOWER BROADWAY)

If you end up on Broadway—and you will—Robert's Western World is the real deal. There's no need to waste your time at the spots with a famous singer's name on the sign. Joshua Hedley has a standing gig at Robert's on Monday nights (when he's not touring), and you're not going to find anything more authentic. The Recession Special—a fried bologna sandwich, chips, a Moon Pie, and a PBR—cures what ails you for just $6. You won't find a better deal downtown.

RUDY'S JAZZ ROOM (THE GULCH)

If you want to put away the cowboy boots for a night and sit out the next line dance, Rudy's Jazz Room offers a sophisticated jazz club experience and welcomes some of the finest players in the world. The space also has a New Orleans–inspired menu, featuring late-night bites like the crawfish grilled cheese and fries and red beans and rice.

SANTA'S PUB (WEDGEWOOD-HOUSTON)

No visit to the Music City is complete without a stop at a karaoke bar, and this double-wide trailer decorated for the holidays year-round reigns supreme. Kacey Musgraves worked there. Ed Sheeran stopped by after a sold-out show at Bridgestone Arena to belt out a One Direction song. And owner Denzel "Santa" Irwin is always happy to regale you with tales of his other celebrity friends—from Brothers Osborne to Kid Rock. There are three important rules at Santa's, though: you can't take your drink on stage, there's no cussin', and it's cash only.

BLAKE ELLS'S NASHVILLE PLAYLIST

Sure, most of the artists you associate with Nashville moved to town from elsewhere to make it big in country music. But a lot of them already lived there, and there's a lot more to Nashville than country music. Cranking it up for a rooftop experience tonight? Lean on Nashville's own Kesha and Young Buck. Angry about an ex? So is Nashville's Paramore. Getting dragged to the bright lights of Broadway? Let Grand Ole Opry legends "Whisperin'" Bill Anderson and Kitty Wells set the mood. And if the night is over and you find yourself hopeless and alone, Nashville native Jelly Roll can relate.

Kitty Wells: "It Wasn't God Who Made Honky Tonk Angels"
Bill Anderson: "Bright Lights and Country Music"
Tom T Hall: "I Like Beer"
Old Crow Medicine Show: "Wagon Wheel"
Justin Townes Earle: "Champagne Corolla"
Loretta Lynn (featuring Jack White): "Portland, Oregon"
Todd Snider: "Nashville"
John Prine: "When I Get to Heaven"
Kings of Leon: "Back Down South"
Jelly Roll: "Save Me"
Gabe Lee: "Buffalo Road"
Joshua Hedley: "Mr. Jukebox"
Paramore: "Misery Business"
Young Buck: "Stay Fly"
Kesha: "Tik Tok"

DOWNTOWN/LOWER BROADWAY

CRAZY TOWN

RHINESTONE COWBOY

SMOKED MAPLE OLD FASHIONED

CADE'S COVE

WHITE PEACH SANGRIA

SMASHVILLE MULE

BRIDESMAID'S TEARS

L & N

ONE PIECE AT A TIME

Ah, the "HonkyTonk Highway" (aka Lower Broadway)—where shall we start? The neon sign–drenched short stretch of road rings loud with competing live bands and soulful twang, inevitable "woos" from passing party buses, and the pitter-patter of cowboy boots clomping up and down the sidewalks. World renowned for the iconic, multilevel honky-tonks and bars where the music, beer, and whiskey all flow like the Cumberland River, more than 14 million people visited downtown Nashville in 2022. If you're looking for a peaceful escape and a short wait time for a drink, I suggest checking out another Nashville neighborhood. As far as Lower Broadway drinks go, at many places you're safest to order a beer or a shot, as the masses make it tough for anyone to craft a proper drink.

With longtime icons like Tootsie's Orchid Lounge, Layla's Honky Tonk, and Robert's Western World surviving the test of time, Nashville's tourist destination essence lies on this strip. At most any of these venues, you'll toast with a holler and swaller and hear world-class musicians perform 365 days a year from 10 a.m. until 3 a.m., so you can honky-tonk (the verb) to your heart's content, usually with no cover charge required.

TENN

GATHER & SHARE

CINNAMON SUGAR BISCUITS | 9
Chocolate Gravy, Berries, Peanuts

DEVILED EGGS | 11
Garlic Chili Crisp, Chive

FRIED GREEN TOMATOES | 15
Whipped Feta, Bacon Jam

BISCUIT SITUATION

FRENCH TOAST | 16
Blueberry Compote, Buttermilk Syrup

FRIED CHICKEN | 18
Pimento Cheese, Hot Honey, Breakfast Potatoes

LOCAL BACON | 16
Scrambled Egg, White Cheddar, Tomato Jam,
Breakfast Potatoes

SOCK SAUSAGE GR
Black P

FRIED GREEN TOMATOES
Whipped Feta, Fig Jam, Arugula, Br

FISCHFR
Over Easy Eg

CRAZY TOWN

BAR TENN AT HOLSTON HOUSE
118 7TH AVENUE NORTH

With a name from a song frequently heard blaring from cover bands on Lower Broadway, this one's a riff on an Irish coffee from Bethany Branfort, using all local ingredients. Using Jack Daniel's instead of Jameson really lets its Tennessee heritage shine.

GLASSWARE: Collins glass

- **Cold brew coffee, as needed**
- **1½ oz. Jack Daniel's Old No. 7**
- **½ oz. honey**
- **½ oz. half-and-half**

1. Fill a collins glass with ice.

2. Add your choice of cold brew to about three-fourths of the way full in your glass.

3. Combine the remaining ingredients in a cocktail shaker.

4. Add ice and shake until the shaker is cold to the touch.

5. Strain the cocktail on top of the cold brew.

TENN

SHARE

...NAMON SUGAR BISCUITS ...
...Chocolate Gravy, Bacon Peanut ...

...DEVILED EGGS | 17
...Chili Crisp, Chive

...EEN TOMATOES | 1...
...Pea, Bacon Jam

...EN TOMATOES | 15
..., Arugula, Breakfast Potatoes

...'S SAUSAGE | 17
...d Paprika Aioli, Breakfast Potat...

...EAR CREEK PATTY | 19
...ese, Bacon Jam, Over Medium Egg,
...Breakfast Potatoes

THINGS

SOUTHERN SUNRISE BREAKFAST | 20
Over Easy Eggs, Fried Peaches, Buttermilk Biscuit,
Sock Sausage Gravy, Breakfast Potatoes

GG WHITE SOUFFLE OMELET | 16
Tomato Verde, Pickled Corn, Goat Cheese,
Choice of Salad or Fruit

COUNTRY HAM CROQUE MADAME |
Peach Mustard, Asiago Bechamel, Sunnyside Egg,
Choice of Salad or Fruit

RHINESTONE COWBOY

Bethany Branfort's original iteration of this cocktail at Bar TENN used Sailor Jerry's for more of a play on tiramisu, but the local whiskey and espresso give more of that kick to help the tourists last all night for any Nashville shows or their nights on Broadway. If you can't get espresso, substitute with dark roast coffee.

GLASSWARE: Mug

GARNISH: Vanilla Whipped Cream (see recipe)

- 1 oz. Nelson's Green Brier Tennessee Whiskey
- 1 oz. Disaronno Originale
- Double shot of espresso

1. In a mug, pour in the whiskey and amaretto liqueur.

2. Prepare your espresso and drip it directly into your mug.

3. Garnish with a generous amount of Vanilla Whipped Cream to your preference.

VANILLA WHIPPED CREAM: Add 2 oz. vanilla syrup and 14 oz. whipping cream directly into a whipped cream dispenser and shake. If you don't have a dispenser, place the ingredients into a mixing bowl and whip using a whisk.

SMOKED MAPLE OLD FASHIONED

BAR TENN AT HOLSTON HOUSE
118 7TH AVENUE NORTH

Found at Holston House's rooftop bar, Heirloom (a nod to the building's long history, complete with a penthouse garden), Bethany Branfort's Smoked Maple Old Fashioned plays off the classic pairing of maple and bacon, but using local country ham with an in-house smoked maple syrup.

GLASSWARE: Rocks glass

GARNISH: Candied Country Ham (see recipe)

- **2 oz. Nelson's Green Brier Tennessee Whiskey**

- **1 oz. Smoked Maple Syrup (see recipe)**

- **3 dashes Angostura bitters**

1. In a mixing glass, add the whiskey, smoked maple syrup, and bitters.

2. Add ice and stir until chilled.

3. Strain into your favorite rocks glass with a large ice cube.

4. Garnish with a piece of Candied Country Ham.

SMOKED MAPLE SYRUP: In a smoker with applewood chips, smoke real maple syrup for 3 to 5 hours.

CANDIED COUNTRY HAM: Thinly slice a hunk of country ham and dip the slices in a thin simple syrup. Dehydrate the slices for a minimum of 5 hours.

CADE'S COVE

HARRIET'S ROOFTOP, 1 HOTEL NASHVILLE
710 DEMONBREUN STREET

Harriet's Rooftop is a 21+ hot spot, perched atop the luxe 1 Hotel Nashville. Beverage manager Harrison Deakin leads the charge with lots of local-inspired sips, both boozy and spirit free. Cade's Cove marries beloved Tennessee whiskey with a sweet-and-sour punch of blackberry jam—they use jam from the Nashville Jam Company.

GLASSWARE: **Rocks glass**

GARNISH: **Blackberries, mint leaves**

- 1½ oz. Uncle Nearest 1856 Premium Aged Whiskey
- ¾ oz. fresh lemon juice
- ⅜ oz. Italicus Rosolio di Bergamotto
- ⅜ oz. blackberry jam
- 3 dashes Peychaud's bitters
- 5 mint leaves
- 2 oz. ginger beer

1. Combine all of the ingredients, except for the ginger beer, in a shaker tin with ice and shake.

2. Strain the cocktail into a rocks glass over the ginger beer and ice.

3. Garnish with fresh, local blackberries and mint leaves.

WHITE PEACH SANGRIA

NUDIE'S HONKY TONK
409 BROADWAY

L et's go, girls! The White Peach Sangria is a refreshing summer-time drink. It's the perfect drink to beat the heat, while hanging out on Nudie's Honky Tonk rooftop bar enjoying the views of downtown Nashville. The bachelorettes are what really inspired the team at Nudie's to make this drink, of course. It's a quick, easy, refreshing drink to make for a crowd. This drink is semisweet with a crisp finish and will have your whole party hurryin' right on back for another one. Adjust the ingredient amounts per personal preference and gussy this recipe up with whatever fruits your heart desire.

✳

GLASSWARE: Wineglass or 16 oz. cup

GARNISH: Freshly sliced peaches

- **4 (750 ml) bottles chardonnay**
- **4 (12 oz.) cans Sprite**
- **1 cup peach schnapps**

1. In a large punch bowl, combine all of the ingredients.

2. Garnish with peaches.

www.theacmenashville.com

SMASHVILLE MULE

ACME FEED & SEED
101 BROADWAY

I f you're never had a Tennessee Mule, it's a nod to the Moscow Mule, made, yes, like it sounds—with Tennessee whiskey. Smashable before or after a Nashville Preds game at the Lower Broadway multilevel bar.

GLASSWARE: 12 oz. plastic cup

GARNISH: Lemon wedge

- 1½ oz. Nelson's Green Brier Tennessee Whiskey
- ¾ oz. fresh lemon juice
- Ginger beer, to top

1. Combine the whiskey and lemon juice over ice in a 12 oz. plastic cup.

2. Top with ginger beer and garnish with a lemon wedge.

BRIDESMAID'S TEARS

ACME FEED & SEED
101 BROADWAY

In case you've been living under a rock, Nashville is one of the country's most popular bachelorette party destinations. Therefore, it's no surprise to find plenty of cheeky pokes at last-minute bridal bashes on drink menus all over town. Here at Acme Feed & Seed's rooftop, Erica Stratton's sweet drink begins with Nashville's own Pickers Vodka—and will come served in a plastic 12 oz. cup (for the safety of bachelorettes and us all, no doubt).

GLASSWARE: 12 oz. plastic cup

GARNISH: Lemon wedge

- **1½ oz. Pickers Pink Lemon Vodka**
- **½ oz. simple syrup**
- **¼ oz. black raspberry liqueur**
- **¼ oz. fresh lemon juice**
- **Lemon-lime soda, to top**

1. Add all of the ingredients to a plastic 12 oz. cup over ice.

2. Top with soda to taste and garnish with a lemon wedge.

L & N

Reposado-based L&N is named after the Louisville and Nashville Railroad, which passed through The Union Station from 1900 through 1979. Inside the historic hotel, nods to the L&N can still be found, including relief artwork of Ms. Louisville and Ms. Nashville 1900 on the south end of the lobby on the fifth floor, as well as a relief sculpture of a Bully 108, a modern steam engine that serviced The Union Station. The Union Station Nashville Yards Hotel's newly revamped flagship spot, ERGO, honors the 120-year history of its home with vibes and drinks like this one, inspired by the romance of rail stations and magnetism of adventure.

GLASSWARE: Coupe glass

GARNISH: Orange peel

- 1½ oz. Cincoro Reposado Tequila
- ¾ oz. Basil Honey Syrup (see recipe)
- 2 dashes Angostura bitters
- Mole bitters, to taste

1. Combine all of the ingredients in a cocktail shaker, add ice, and shake vigorously.

2. Strain the cocktail into a coupe.

3. Garnish with an orange peel.

BASIL HONEY SYRUP: Add 1 bunch of basil leaves, ½ cup water, ½ cup honey, and a pinch sea salt to a blender and blend until smooth. Strain the syrup through a fine-mesh strainer and use.

LOUISVILLE & NASHVILLE R. R. CO.
SHOW SCRIP
Subject to Conditions of Contract
VOID IF DETACHED 5926 FORM S. S. B.
VALUE 1¢   BAGGAGE

ONE PIECE AT A TIME

Taking its name from one of Johnny Cash's songs, this refreshing cocktail is Tennessee whiskey–based, semisweet, and easy to enjoy.

❋

GLASSWARE: Martini glass or 12 oz. cup

GARNISH: Lemon wedge

- **1½ oz. George Dickel Classic Recipe**
- **1 oz. fresh lemon juice**
- **Ginger ale, to top**

1. Combine all of the ingredients, except for the ginger ale, in a mixing glass and stir.

2. Pour the mixture over ice into a martini glass or 12 oz. cup and top with ginger ale.

3. Garnish with a lemon wedge.

PRINTERS ALLEY

THE DUKE

QUARTER TANK OF GASOLINE

NO TRUE SCOTSMAN

REAPPEARING ACT

SOME LUCKY DAY

J ust off the beaten path of Lower Broadway, tucked between Third Avenue and Fourth Avenue and running from Union Street to Commerce Street in downtown Nashville, is Printers Alley. The name comes from Nashville's connection to the printing and publishing industries—at the start of the twentieth century, the alley was home to two large newspapers, ten print shops, and thirteen publishers. Even as late as the 1960s, Nashville was home to over thirty-six printing companies.

Let's not forget that Printers Alley was, and still is, more than the clatter of the presses and the clinking of glasses. It's also the sound of music echoing off of century-old brick walls, the laughter and chatter from patrons spilling out into the night, and the murmur of secrets shared under hushed tones.

The part of the alley that runs between Union and Church celebrated its heyday as a nightclub district in the1940s, a true nightlife hub servicing the restaurants and hotels along Fourth Avenue, which became known as the "men's quarter." When the nightclubs opened, the alley became a place where performers like Chet Atkins, Waylon Jennings, Hank Williams, and Dottie West made their mark. During this time, the sale of liquor for consumption on premises was illegal in Nashville. However, the story goes that establishments in Printers Alley served it anyway, claiming it was the "brown-bagged" thirsty customers who brought the booze.

It was an era when the adventurous would slip through secret entrances, and the alley was alive with tantalizing burlesque performances, electrifying live music, and high-stakes games of chance.

Today, the printing presses may have ceased their hum, but the likes of The Black Poodle Lounge, The Carousel Club, and The Rainbow Room ensure that Printers Alley still echoes with a rich and vibrant history.

BAR SPOTLIGHT: SKULL'S RAINBOW ROOM

222 PRINTERS ALLEY

One place and one place only has been the cornerstone of Printers Alley since 1948, when David "Skull" Schulman originally opened The Rainbow Room. Artists such as Elvis Presley, Patsy Cline, Johnny Cash, Bob Dylan, and many more have entertained audiences from the checkerboard stage of this venue, located in the basement of the historic Southern Turf Building.

A semiregular cast member on the *Hee-Haw* television series who liked to wear his faded blue overalls from the show behind the bar, Schulman was so beloved by Nashvillians that the Nashville City Council declared him "The Mayor of Printers Alley." Originally, The Rainbow Room was an exotic dance club that "Skull" eventually converted to a country bar in the 1990s. Prior to the transition, the club was the only venue in Nashville with a live band performing music for its dancers.

Tragically, one night in 1998, Schulman was attacked and murdered by two assailants while working alone at the club. The killers were eventually caught, but the club didn't reopen. A neighboring Printers Alley bar rented the space for storage for a while, but no employees wanted to enter—many visitors claimed to have seen a shape resembling Skull walking around the club and could hear his voice calling out to them.

The bar sat shuttered for nearly two decades after Schulman's murder but reopened in 2015 as Skull's Rainbow Room as a tribute to Schulman. Now one of the best dining and drinking spots in the Alley, you can still find some of the best live jazz nightly, and late-night burlesque shows on Thursday, Friday, and Saturday nights on the original checkerboard stage.

THE DUKE

SKULL'S RAINBOW ROOM
222 PRINTERS ALLEY

There are two kinds of worries," Edward Kennedy Ellington, aka Duke, said, "those you can do something about and those you can't. Don't spend any time on the latter." Skull's classic cocktail, whose name comes from the famous big band and jazz pioneer who was always seen with a cigar on stage, strives to embody that mantra in a ragtime, bebop-inspired recipe. Duke played in Nashville many times throughout his career, most famously at The Silver Streak, which was located right off Broadway. Skull's Rainbow Room's play on a classic Old Fashioned is a Dixieland fusion of tobacco bitters, sage-infused simple syrup, and garnish. These flavors make a splash on the palate that will have you tapping your foot to the swing beat of a drum and smiling as wide as Duke himself.

GLASSWARE: Lowball glass

GARNISH: Sage leaf, lemon peel

- ½ oz. Sage Simple Syrup (see recipe)
- 2 oz. Nelson Brothers Classic Bourbon
- 2 dashes tobacco bitters
- 2 dashes Angostura bitters

1. In a lowball glass, add three large ice cubes.
2. Make an "all together now" pour of sage syrup and whiskey at proper counts.
3. Make an "A 1-2-3-4" count of tobacco and Angostura bitters.
4. Garnish with a single sage leaf and a lemon peel.

SAGE SIMPLE SYRUP: In a small saucepan over medium heat, combine 1 cup water and 1 cup sugar and stir until the sugar is dissolved. Remove the simple syrup from heat and steep 10 sage leaves in it for at least 10 minutes. Strain the syrup and allow it to cool.

BAR SPOTLIGHT: BLACK RABBIT

218 3RD AVENUE NORTH

Nestled on the ground floor of a historic building dating back to the late 1800s, chef-owner Trey Cioccia's cocktail den beckons with live piano, Southern blues, or live jazz, depending on what night of the week you visit. The bar's exposed brick walls, soaring ceilings, and original pine floors speak of the building's history, whispering tales of days long gone. However, it's the dimly lit corners and sumptuous velvet booths that truly encapsulate the opulence and allure of the clandestine speakeasies that flourished during the Prohibition Era. It's a place where history dances with fantasy, and where the heartbeat of Nashville's old nightclub district continues to pulse today.

QUARTER TANK OF GASOLINE

BLACK RABBIT
218 3RD AVENUE NORTH

This cocktail was born when Tommy Hartzog, Black Rabbit's managing partner, wanted to feature a drink that reminded him of the sassafras tea his father would sip in his rocking chair on the front porch—that was his father's way of winding down after a long day working in the yard in Mt. Juliet, Tennessee. The result is this light and refreshing take on a Whiskey Smash. The name has a double meaning. First, it's the title of a song by one of Hartzog's favorite songwriters, Daniel Hutchens (Bloodkin), who passed away the weekend before the cocktail debuted. Second, the Nelson brothers, of the local Nelson's Green Brier Distillery, discovered the location of their ancestors' nineteenth-century distillery serrendipitously: they were headed out into the countryside and had gotten down to a—you guessed it—quarter tank of gasoline. So they stopped at a service station in Green Brier, Tennessee.

GLASSWARE: **Rocks glass**

GARNISH: **Mint sprig**

- **2 oz. Nelson's Green Brier Tennessee Whiskey**
- **1 oz. Sassafras Syrup (see recipe)**
- **½ oz. fresh lemon juice**

1. Combine all of the ingredients in a cocktail shaker and shake with ice.

2. Strain the cocktail over ice into a rocks glass.

3. Garnish with a sprig of mint.

SASSAFRAS SYRUP:
In a mixing glass, muddle
3 sprigs of mint and the
zest of 2 lemons with 12 oz.
simple syrup. Add 12 oz.
sassafras tea concentrate
and stir or shake to incorporate. Refrigerate over-
night before use.

CHRISTEN MCCLURE, HOUSE OF CARDS AND SINATRA BAR & LOUNGE

Christen McClure knows what she is doing, and she has fun doing it. As much a storyteller as she is an expert at her craft, Christen shares a cheeky (and oh-so-Nashville) story of how she got to where she is today—beverage director at Sinatra Bar & Lounge and House of Cards—and tells us the stories behind a few of her cocktail recipes. Here she is in her own words.

HOW TO BECOME A BEVERAGE DIRECTOR IN FOUR EASY STEPS

STEP ONE

Wait tables because you think you're going to be a professional musician.

STEP TWO

Quickly catch on to how much more money you can make when you talk to guests about wine, and then how much MORE money you can make when you actually know what you're talking about.

STEP THREE

Annoy every chef you've ever worked for by asking 10,000 questions about how flavors work.

STEP FOUR

Think about joining a culinary program, admit that you hate being sweaty on a hot line, and get behind the bar instead.

BEHIND THE COCKTAIL: NO TRUE SCOTSMAN

SINATRA BAR
222 4TH AVENUE NORTH

"This is a nod to a classic but often forgotten gin Martini called the Gibson, which is identical in every way to a dry gin Martini except for one crucial ingredient—the humble pickled pearl onion," says Christen McClure.

"Like most bar lore, this cocktail's origins are dubious at best. Some say Charles Dana Gibson (of Gibson Girl drawings fame) asked his local bartender to improve his 50/50 gin Martini and the faithful knight of the brass rail answered the call—by cheekily dropping a pickled onion into his glass. Some say a relatively anonymous San Francisco businessman named Gibson believed onions could prevent the common cold, and we know a spoonful of gin helps the medicine go down! We do know no published recipe called for the onion until after Prohibition, and that's just fine with us.

"I created this cocktail as an homage to my immigrant father—he emigrated from Scotland in the 1970s and his cocktail of choice will forever be the Gibson, although he prefers them on the rocks and as cold as chemically possible. I've listened to him complain about American bars not keeping pickled onions on hand my entire life, and I promised him I would try to give them a home if I ever got the chance.

"I use a distinctly Scottish gin, The Botanist Islay Dry Gin, made by our friends at Bruichladdich Distillery. It captures the terroir of Islay, Scotland—exceptionally herbaceous and green with wood sage, water mint, and thyme. All perfectly balanced with hearty florals like chamomile, sweet gale, and gorse. This complexity is reinforced by a decidedly New School dry vermouth from Lo-Fi Aperitifs, featuring beautiful California fruit. I love its unique freshness, and gentle dryness. It reinforces some of my favorite flavors from The Botanist, including chamomile and citrus, with a distinctive gentian root running through its heart.

"I've had the honor of working with some of the best chefs in the world, so I know all these flavors can absolutely be grounded with just a touch of salt and acid, and the tiniest dash of olive brine is not traditional by any means, but it operates like a sprinkle of Maldon sea salt in the glass. I also chose just a tiny bit of complex and vegetal celery bitters from Berg & Hauck simply to reinforce the true savory nature of this cocktail. It's presented in honor of my father, Matthew McClure, and is sure to delight anyone who wants to make a departure from the sweet and fruity that dominates contemporary cocktail culture.

NO TRUE SCOTSMAN

SINATRA BAR
222 4TH AVENUE NORTH

C hristen McClure's take on The Gibson pays homage to her father, who immigrated from Scotland.

GLASSWARE: Rocks glass

GARNISH: 1 to 3 pickled cocktail onions

- 2 oz. The Botanist Islay Dry Gin
- 1 oz. Lo-Fi Aperitifs Dry Vermouth
- ¼ oz. olive brine
- 2 dashes Berg & Hauck's Original Celery Bitters

1. Combine all of the ingredients in a shaker tin, add a scoop of ice, and shake for 15 seconds.

2. Strain the cocktail into a rocks glass and add half a scoop of fresh ice.

3. Garnish with the pickled cocktail onions.

BEHIND THE COCKTAIL: REAPPEARING ACT

HOUSE OF CARDS
LOWER LEVEL, 119 3RD AVENUE SOUTH

"This is a cocktail so nice I had to name it twice!" says Christen McClure. "It was placed at House of Cards in 2020 under the name "Disappearing Act," because it was designed to be so perfectly crushable it would literally disappear. It ran its course through a summer season and was replaced with a more winter-weighted tequila offering. I have never been prouder to receive hate mail in my entire career. I didn't realize it was such a fan favorite until it was gone, but our guests were extremely vocal with their feedback so when I brought it back, I couldn't resist renaming it "Reappearing Act." This amped-up Margarita is a fantastic example of the anarchist-collective approach I always try to offer to my bar teams—anyone can work on anything they want and all parties, myself included, are available to collaborate.

"I had a bartender, Clay Franklin, with a background in gastronomy who wanted to bring an oleo saccharum into the mix. This sounds much fancier than it is—it's essentially an infusion of citrus oils into salt and/or sugar that can then be made into a syrup. Knowing we were working toward a Margarita, we opted for both sugar and salt over sweet Meyer lemon peels to build that satisfying salt-and-silver-tequila quality right into the glass. Once we had the essential elements of a classic Margarita—tequila, salt, and citrus—it was time to take it to the next level.

"Everyone agreed it deserved a little bit of extra complexity, and, since we have such an incredible wine program at House of Cards, it made perfect sense to incorporate some of our favorite white wines as well. It's also a great way to use up a home bottle that's lost some of its delightfulness after opening but hasn't turned. As the late, great Julia Child often said, never cook with a wine you wouldn't drink.

"Finally, lemon and berry have always had a natural flavor affinity, and cassis brings a fruitiness that isn't too sweet and has an especially dark aspect that gives the cocktail its mysterious, layered effect. The final result is a lemon-berry Margarita that is greater than the sum of its parts: sweet, tangy, salty, and strong."

REAPPEARING ACT

Christen McClure's elevated take on the Margarita is decked out with complexity and flavor. The ripe balance provided by the cassis shines at first sip of this salty, citrusy, and sweet tequila showstopper.

GLASSWARE: 15 oz. brandy snifter

- 1½ oz. Lunazul Tequila Blanco
- 1 oz. freshly squeezed lime juice
- ¾ oz. Meyer Lemon Oleo Saccharum (see recipe)

- ¾ oz. White Wine Syrup (see recipe)
- ½ oz. Torres Magdala Orange Liqueur
- ½ oz. Giffard Crème de Cassis d'Anjou

1. Combine all of the ingredients, except for the crème de cassis, in a shaker tin and dry-shake without ice for 10 seconds to combine.

2. In a 15 oz. brandy snifter, add the crème de cassis and fill the snifter with crushed ice.

3. Pour the shaker mixture over the top, slowly, to chill and dilute the mixed cocktail and preserve the layers of deep purple, light purple, fuschia, and yellow.

Meyer Lemon Oleo Saccharum: Peel 6 to 8 medium-size Meyer lemons (regular lemons will absolutely do as well). Use a potato peeler to make sure you don't get any of the white pith—it's the essential oils in the bumpy skin you're after. Place the peels into a clean 8 oz. mason jar and cover them with ½ cup white sugar and 3 tablespoons coarse sea salt. Secure the lid and shake to coat. Let this sit in a cool, dry place for 2 to 3 days, shaking the mixture occasionally. The salt and sugar will draw the oils out of the peels, making a thick liquid. After 3 days, add 6 oz. boiling hot water and an additional ½ cup sugar to the jar. Stir until all grains have dissolved. Cool completely, with peels, before using. Discard peels before using. You should have a sweet, lemony syrup left, with a hint of salinity. This mixture will keep for up to 1 week in the refrigerator.

White Wine Syrup: Add 8 oz. white wine—preferably an Italian Gavi or North African sauv blanc—to a small saucepan. One that's been open for a day or two but kept in the fridge is a great choice, as the oxidation will add complexity. Add 1 cup white sugar to the pan. Bring the mixture to a gentle boil. It will smell terrible—there is no way around it. The phenolics of cooking wine will smell like vinegar and you will naturally be concerned but do not panic! Continue to cook until the mixture thickens enough to where it runs off a spoon in a solid ribbon. Remove the syrup from heat and allow it to cool completely before using. It will keep for up to 1 week in the refrigerator.

SOME LUCKY DAY

SINATRA BAR
222 4TH AVENUE NORTH

In 1897, the federal government passed the bottled-in-bond law decreeing that bonded whiskey be made by a single distillery from one distillation season, aged in a bonded warehouse for at least four years, and bottled at exactly 100 proof. Today, whiskeys can consist of blends from multiple growing seasons or sourced from more than one distillery. Jack Daniel's Bonded Tennessee Whiskey has sweet caramel notes zapped with cinnamon and black pepper spice, which Christen McClure takes to the next level at the Sinatra Bar. You can substitute strong coffee for espresso.

GLASSWARE: 12 oz. glass

GARNISH: Cinnamon

- 1½ oz. Jack Daniel's Bonded Tennessee Whiskey
- 2 oz. espresso, cooled
- 1 oz. real maple syrup
- 1½ oz. Vespertino Tequila Crema
- 1 oz. heavy whipping cream

1. In a 12 oz. glass, mix the whiskey and maple syrup with the cooled coffee.
2. Add ice and a straw and give it a swirl.
3. In a separate glass, combine the Vespertino and heavy whipping cream and froth for 15 to 20 seconds, until the mixture thickens but doesn't firm up.
4. Pour the cold foam over the coffee mixture.
5. Garnish with a sprinkle of cinnamon.

THE GULCH, SOBRO,
RUTLEDGE HILL, AND PIE TOWN

OFFICIAL DRINK OF NASHVILLE

STRANGE BREW

SECRET THIRD THING

PORK & STORMY

THE OL' CHAUHAN

POP POP IN THE ATTIC

I SAID GOOD DAY

WE WERE ON A BREAK

404 OLD FASHIONED

VANILLA OLD FASHIONED

PABLO HONEY

17 STEPS FROM RYE-MAN

VIRAGO WASABI MARTINI

SOUTHERN BELLE SOUR

THE OAKFATHER

Like several other Nashville neighborhoods where locals and tourists flock to imbibe, the Gulch wasn't exactly a destination for cocktail sipping just two decades ago. In its former heyday, it served as the site of Nashville's bustling railroad yards, but the area fell into neglect post-World War II.

Named for a natural geographic depression throughout the 110-acre development, the largely ignored Gulch began seeing new life in the early 2000s, and today it is one of the city's most bustling, walkable neighborhoods on weekends. More of a brunchtime haven and less of a late-night kind of neighborhood (as the coffee-centric cocktails that follow can attest), the Gulch provides a balance of bottomless Mimosas, Bloody Marys, and Espresso Martinis fueling hangover-healing brunches and whiskey drinks aplenty for happy hours and dinner drinking options.

Just a stone's throw away (okay, a short walk) to the northeast of the Gulch you'll find small neighborhoods like SoBro (South of Broadway's madness, just like it sounds) and compact Rutledge Hill, which is home to the intimate Listening Room Cafe and longstanding singer-songwriter night destination 3rd and Lindsley, plus the Nashville outpost of Charleston-based Southern food bastion, Husk.

I've thrown in a little sliver of Nashville known as Pie Town for good measure (and Music City importance). This is where Nashville's outpost of Jack White's Third Man Records lives, including a record store, the world's only live venue with direct-to-acetate recording capabilities, and The Blue Room Bar.

OFFICIAL DRINK OF NASHVILLE

L.A. JACKSON
401 11TH AVENUE SOUTH

A creation from popular Gulch rooftop, L.A. Jackson, perched atop The Thompson Nashville hotel, the ODN earned its name when it was crowned the "Official Drink of Nashville" at the 2018 Music City Food and Wine Festival. Originally dubbed "The 615," this cocktail highlights some of Tennessee's greatest local finds as key ingredients. This Whiskey Smash/Whiskey Sour hybrid is a balanced, light drink utilizing Chattanooga Reserve Whiskey and honey from local beekeepers. The mainstream mint garnish is made to stand out with an extra sprinkle of bee pollen on top, also sourced from Nashville's beekeeper community.

GLASSWARE: Collins glass
GARNISH: Mint sprig, bee pollen

- 1½ oz. Chattanooga Reserve Whiskey
- ¾ oz. pineapple juice
- ½ oz. lemon juice
- ½ oz. Aperol
- ¼ oz. curaçao
- ¼ oz. honey
- ¼ oz. Ginger Syrup (see recipe)
- 2 dashes Angostura bitters

1. Combine all of the ingredients in a cocktail shaker and shake.

2. Pour the cocktail into a collins glass and fill with crushed ice.

3. Garnish with a mint sprig and bee pollen.

GINGER SYRUP: In a saucepan on medium heat, combine 1 cup granulated sugar and ¾ cup water. Stir constantly until the sugar is dissolved. Add 1 cup sliced fresh gingerroot, peeled, and continue to heat, bringing the syrup to a light boil. Cover, reduce the heat, and allow the syrup to simmer for about 15 minutes. Remove the pan from heat and allow the syrup to cool and steep in the covered pan for about 1 hour, or until it reaches your preferred taste. Strain out the ginger and bottle under a tight seal.

STRANGE BREW

Husk Nashville's cocktail program, led by Adam Morgan, focuses on using homegrown ingredients and byproducts from its outstanding culinary program. Not veering from their dedication to all things local, Adam's take on the omnipresent Espresso Martini is a caffeinated crowd pleaser, using neighborhood darling Crema coffee alongside sherry and tequila.

GLASSWARE: Nick & Nora glass
GARNISH: Freshly grated nutmeg, edible flower

- 1 oz. tequila
- 1 oz. Mr Black Coffee Amaro
- 1 oz. chilled coffee
- ¼ oz. oloroso sherry
- ½ oz. Coffee Cordial (see recipe)
- Dash Angostura bitters
- Pinch salt

1. Shake all of the ingredients together in a cocktail shaker and strain the cocktail into a Nick & Nora.

2. Grate fresh nutmeg overtop to garnish, and add an edible flower.

COFFEE CORDIAL: Mix equal parts sugar and hot coffee together in a container of your choice. Then add ½ oz. vanilla liqueur to taste.

SECRET THIRD THING

HUSK
37 RUTLEDGE STREET

Husk's baijiu-focused cocktail has recently become a guest favorite. Named for being a "secret third drink" in between a Tiki and a Sour, bar manager Adam Morgan makes his shrub with fresh shiso grown in Husk's backyard garden. For those unfamiliar, baijiu is a family of traditional Chinese grain spirits.

GLASSWARE: Collins glass

GARNISH: Shiso leaf

- 1¼ oz. Ming River Sichuan Baijiu
- ¾ oz. fresh lime juice
- ¾ oz. Watermelon-Shiso Shrub (see recipe)
- ½ oz. Green Chartreuse
- 2 to 3 dashes saline solution
- Sparkling water, to top
- ¾ oz. Underberg bitters, to float

1. In a cocktail shaker, shake all of the ingredients, except for the sparkling water and bitters, with ice.

2. Strain the cocktail over ice into a collins glass.

3. Top with a splash of sparkling water then float the bitters on top.

4. Garnish with a shiso leaf.

WATERMELON-SHISO SHRUB: Combine 2 cups sugar, 1 cup chopped watermelon, and 3 to 4 shiso leaves in a blender and blend on high for 1 minute. Strain the shrub and refrigerate it for up to 2 weeks.

PORK & STORMY

A ward-winning pitmaster Carey Bringle is a Nashville native, with deep roots in the West Tennessee barbecue culture, and his Gulch restaurant, Peg Leg Porker, even has its own private label Tennessee straight bourbon whiskey. Carey's own favorite cocktail, the Pork & Stormy, is their smoky spin on the Moscow Mule, beginning and ending with the nutty sweetness of the bourbon and a hefty squeeze of lime.

GLASSWARE: Rocks glass

GARNISH: Lime wedge

- 2 oz. Peg Leg Porker Tennessee Straight Bourbon Whiskey
- Barritt's Original Ginger Beer, to top
- Squeeze of fresh lime juice

1. Fill a rocks glass with ice to the brim, then add the bourbon.

2. Top with the ginger beer.

3. Add a squeeze of lime juice and garnish with a lime wedge.

THE OL' CHAUHAN

CHAUHAN ALE & MASALA HOUSE
123 12TH AVENUE NORTH

Like an Old Fashioned with a spice queen spin from Nashville-based celebrity chef Maneet Chauhan's eponymous restaurant, The Ol' Chauhan is a great warm-up drink for winter, according to Jen Fuller. Spicy bitters, cardamom, and clove notes all intermingle for flavors that lend a bit toward a booze-infused Cherry Coke.

GLASSWARE: Rocks glass

GARNISH: Orange peel

- 2 oz. Old Forester 86 Proof Bourbon
- ½ oz. Spiced Cold Syrup (see recipe)
- ¼ oz. Amaro Averna
- 3 dashes Woodford Reserve Spiced Cherry Bitters

1. Add all of the ingredients to a mixing glass with ice and stir.

2. Strain the cocktail into a rocks glass with ice.

3. Express an orange peel over the drink and garnish with the peel.

SPICED COLD SYRUP: In a small saucepan over medium heat, combine 1 cup water and 1 cup sugar and bring the mixture to a simmer, stirring until the sugar is dissolved. Remove from heat and add 6 cloves and 2 green cardamom pods and cover the pan. Let the mixture steep for at least 4 hours. Strain before using.

BAR SPOTLIGHT: GERTIE'S WHISKEY BAR

507 12TH AVENUE SOUTH

In the bustling heart of the Gulch, a vibrant orange door leads to Gertie's Whiskey Bar, which hosts a massive wall chock-full of one of the South's most impressive collections of coveted whiskeys.

Located on the first floor of The 404 Kitchen, whiskey lovers gather around the long, curved bar to sample some of America's most sought-after whiskeys—straight up, or in carefully crafted cocktails.

Named for Gertrude Cleo Lythgoe, known as "Queen of the Bootleggers," Gertie's celebrates freethinking and individualism, at the bar and in the glass. Gertie's has garnered much attention for its outstanding collection of over 650 bottles of rare and hard-to-find whiskeys, including many limited edition barrels selected by The 404 Kitchen chef Matt Bolus in partnership with local distillers. Gertie's also offers a distinctive selection of rare and unusual wines, and an expertly curated menu of craft beers.

Pro Tips: At both Gertie's and The 404 Kitchen upstairs, a wildly popular weekly Whiskey Wednesday features select whiskies poured |for half off, all night long. There's also a members-only Whiskey Society that gives exclusive access to some of the team's one-of-a-kind barrel selects.

POP POP IN THE ATTIC

THE 404 KITCHEN/GERTIE'S WHISKEY BAR
507 12TH AVENUE SOUTH

Easily crushable especially in the summertime, according to beverage director Bri Parino, this fun, more constructive take on a Bramble is tart and fruit-forward, yet balanced by the rich quality of the rye and a hint of spice.

GLASSWARE: Rocks glass

GARNISH: Dehydrated lime wheel with powdered sugar

- **2 oz. Rittenhouse Straight Rye Whisky**
- **1 oz. Raspberry Syrup (see recipe)**
- **½ oz. Ginger Syrup (see recipe on page 73)**
- **½ oz. fresh lemon juice**
- **4 dashes rhubarb bitters**

1. In a cocktail tin, combine all of the ingredients.

2. Add ice and shake for 15 to 30 seconds.

3. Strain and pour the cocktail over ice in a rocks glass.

4. Garnish with a dehydrated lime wheel that is half-coated with powdered sugar.

RASPBERRY SYRUP: In a small saucepan over medium heat, combine 1 cup raspberries, 1 cup water, 1 cup sugar, and 2 tablespoons fresh lemon juice and stir until the sugar is dissolved. Remove the mixture from heat and muddle the raspberries to release their juices. Allow the syrup to cool then strain it before use.

I SAID GOOD DAY

THE 404 KITCHEN/GERTIE'S WHISKEY BAR
507 12TH AVENUE SOUTH

This bright and peppery tropical-inspired sunshine in a glass begins with Nashville's own Pickers Original Vodka," says Bri Parino. "It harmonizes both sweet and spicy with notes of tree nut and bitter orange."

GLASSWARE: Collins glass

GARNISH: Edible flower, chile lollipop

- 1½ oz. Pickers Original Vodka
- 1 oz. Strawberry-Infused Aperol (see recipe)
- ½ oz. orgeat
- ½ oz. Giffard Piment d'Espelette Liqueur
- ½ oz. fresh lemon juice

1. In a cocktail tin, add all of the ingredients.

2. Add ice and shake for 15 seconds

3. Strain the cocktail over an ice spear in a collins glass and garnish with an edible flower and chile lollipop.

STRAWBERRY-INFUSED APEROL: Combine 1 (750 ml) bottle of Aperol and 1 cup (or more or less, as desired) strawberries, stemmed and quatered, and refrigerate for 24 hours. Strain before using.

WE WERE ON A BREAK

This intriguing, complex cocktail leans on prominent root flavors with prickly pear to lighten it up, says Bri Parino. "The *Friends*-inspired name has the same mood as this fun sipping cocktail—moody, yet playful." Bordeaux cherries can be used instead of pickled blueberries for the garnish.

GLASSWARE: Coupe glass

GARNISH: 3 pickled blueberries on a skewer

- 1½ oz. Condesa Prickly Pear & Orange Blossom Gin
- 1 oz. prickly pear liqueur
- 1 butterfly pea flower sugar cube
- ½ oz. fresh lemon juice

1. In a cocktail tin, combine all of the ingredients (including sugar cube: we want that to break down while we shake).

2. Add ice and shake for 30 seconds

3. Strain the cocktail into a fancy coupe and garnish with pickled blueberries on a skewer.

404 OLD FASHIONED

THE 404 KITCHEN/GERTIE'S WHISKEY BAR
507 12TH AVENUE SOUTH

Matt Bolus, executive chef/partner of The 404 Kitchen and Gertie's Whiskey Bar, designed everything in the upstairs/downstairs restaurant and bar with the South in mind. So when their consulting mixologist started looking at flavors like pecans, apples, and butter when creating a signature Old Fashioned, Bolus's first instinct was that they were poking fun at southerners by using butter. After tasting the brown butter Old Fashioned, however, all other versions were ruined for the chef forever. "It's like butter and bourbon are ageless lovers," he says.

GLASSWARE: Rocks glass

GARNISH: Dried apple slice

- 2 oz. Brown Butter Bourbon (see recipe)

- ½ oz. Pecan Simple Syrup (see recipe)

- Dash Angostura bitters

1. Add all of the ingredients to a mixing glass and add ice.

2. Stir for 15 to 25 seconds.

3. Strain the cocktail over a large ice cube into a rocks glass.

4. Garnish with a dried apple slice.

BROWN BUTTER BOURBON: Heat Plugrà Butter, to taste, on low heat and let it brown, stirring occasionally. Add the browned butter to a bottle of bourbon and let the mixture infuse for 1 to 2 days.

PECAN SIMPLE SYRUP: In a small saucepan, toast 1 cup pecans over medium-low heat for 3 minutes. Add 1 cup water and 1 cup sugar, raise the heat to medium, and stir until the sugar is dissolved. Remove the syrup from heat, allow it to cool, and strain before using.

VANILLA OLD FASHIONED

KAYNE PRIME
1103 MCGAVOCK STREET

Nashville-based hospitality group M Street was one of the earliest pioneers of the Gulch neighborhood. At this steak house with a happening bar, Kayne Prime offers a sweeter take on the classic with vanilla syrup. It's a crowd favorite.

GLASSWARE: Rocks glass

GARNISH: Orange peel

- 1½ oz. Chattanooga Whiskey 91
- ½ oz. Amaro Nonino Quintessentia
- ¼ oz. Vanilla Simple Syrup (see recipe)
- 2 dashes Regans' Orange Bitters
- Dash Angostura bitters

1. Combine all of the ingredients in a mixing glass with ice and stir.

2. Strain the cocktail over a large ice cube into a rocks glass.

3. Express an orange peel over the cocktail and add the peel as a garnish.

VANILLA SIMPLE SYRUP: In a small saucepan over medium heat, combine 1 cup water and 1 cup sugar and stir until the sugar is dissolved. Remove the simple syrup from heat and add 1 vanilla bean, cut in half lengthwise (or ½ tablespoon vanilla extract), and stir. Allow the syrup to cool, and remove the bean before using.

PABLO HONEY

S aint Añejo tips its hat to Midtown's former brunch destination Tavern (also from the M Street Restaurant Group) with this beloved cocktail from its now-shuttered sister restaurant. The flavors fit well with the Mexican food on offer. Pair with plenty of salsa, queso, and guac and sip carefully, as it goes down easily.

GLASSWARE: Rocks glass

GARNISH: Lime wedge

- **2 oz. Lunazul Tequila Blanco**
- **½ oz. fresh lime juice**

- **½ oz. Blackberry Reàl Blackberry Puree Infused Syrup**

1. Combine all of the ingredients in a cocktail shaker with ice and shake.

2. Strain the cocktail over ice into a rocks glass.

3. Garnish with a lime wedge.

17 STEPS FROM RYE-MAN

MIMO RESTAURANT AND BAR
100 DEMONBREUN STREET

F olks say that artists were able to discreetly leave the Ryman Tabernacle during breaks between performances to visit a nearby bar in a tradition that dates back to the early 1900s. It is said that this was accomplished in just seventeen steps. This unique drink showcases local ingredients and features the citrusy and hoppy flavors that define it. The combination of the spicy yet fruity rye whiskey with the hops and citrus notes of the IPA creates a complex yet inviting experience enticing you to never run dry.

GLASSWARE: Martini glass

GARNISH: Grapefruit peel

- 1½ oz. George Dickel Rye
- ¾ oz. Ginger Syrup (see recipe on page 73)
- ½ oz. Cointreau
- ½ oz. fresh lime juice
- 1 oz. Bearded Iris Brewing Homestyle IPA, to top

1. Combine all of the ingredients, except for the beer, in a shaker tin.

2. Add ice and shake.

3. Double-strain the cocktail into a martini glass.

4. Top with the beer and express a grapefruit peel over the drink, then place the peel on the rim.

VIRAGO WASABI MARTINI

VIRAGO
1120 MCGAVOCK STREET

A t M Street's swanky sushi spot, Virago, a classic gets a spicy upgrade with wasabi simple syrup. Though the restaurant has relocated a few times, this signature drink remains a constant and kicks off a sushi meal with a bang.

✳

GLASSWARE: Coupe glass

GARNISH: Dehydrated lemon wheel

- 2 oz. Finlandia Classic Vodka
- ¾ oz. fresh lime juice
- ¾ oz. Wasabi Simple Syrup (see recipe)

1. Combine all of the ingredients in a cocktail shaker with ice and shake.

2. Strain the cocktail into a coupe.

3. Garnish with a dehydrated lemon wheel.

WASABI SIMPLE SYRUP: In a small saucepan over medium heat, combine 1 cup water, 1 cup sugar, and 1 to 2 barspoons raw wasabi powder or wasabi paste, depending on your spice preference, and stir until the sugar and wasabi have dissolved. Remove the syrup from heat, let it cool completely, and refrigerate it before using.

SOUTHERN BELLE SOUR

OAK STEAKHOUSE NASHVILLE
801 CLARK PLACE

The Oak Steakhouse, located in the Westin Nashville, pays homage to the bartending traditions of the nineteenth century. This bourbon-forward sour packs a tangy, fruity punch that is softened by foamed egg white and the slightly toffee flavor of the demerara simple syrup. A little bit spicy and a little bit sweet, much like its namesake, don't you think?

GLASSWARE: Rocks glass

GARNISH: Cherry

- 2 oz. Buffalo Trace Bourbon
- 1 oz. fresh lemon juice
- ¾ oz. demerara simple syrup
- ½ oz. egg white
- 3 dashes peach bitters
- Cherry juice, to mist
- Blackberry juice, to mist

1. Combine all of the ingredients, except for the cherry and blackberry juices, in a cocktail shaker with ice and shake hard.

2. Strain the cocktail over a big ice cube into a rocks glass.

3. Spray 4 spritzes of a mixture of cherry juice and blackberry juice.

4. Garnish with a cherry.

THE OAKFATHER

OAK STEAKHOUSE NASHVILLE
801 CLARK PLACE

From bar manager Josh Johnson, the Oakfather is a riff on the classic Godfather cocktail.

GLASSWARE: Snifter glass

GARNISH: Cherry and lemon peel on a skewer

- 1 oz. Talisker 10 Year Old Single Malt Scotch Whisky
- ¾ oz. amaretto liqueur
- ½ oz. Green Chartreuse
- ½ oz. Vanilla Simple Syrup (see recipe on page 93)
- ½ oz. fresh lemon juice

1. Combine all of the ingredients in a cocktail shaker with ice and shake.

2. Serve in a snifter glass and garnish with a cherry on a skewer with a lemon peel.

MIDTOWN/MUSIC ROW/
EDGEHILL

TOMCAT SOUR

PRESIDENTIAL SUITE

BLOOD AND SAND

PAPER CHAMPION

GRIFFIN'S DECEPTION

IT'S ONLY FOREVER

LADY STARDUST

A MILLION THINGS TO SAY

THE GREAT BAMBINO

A trio of neighborhoods best known for recording studios, publishing houses, and music video production, as well as a world-class hospital and school of medicine (not to mention the famous "naked people" statue at the traffic circle), the Midtown, Music Row, and Edgehill section of Nashville is a bit of a cocktail of neighborhoods in its own right. Here, Vanderbilt students and doctors mingle with songwriters and singers from Music Row—"where the music is made, not played," as I tell tourists so they don't confuse Music Row with the Lower Broadway honky-tonks.

While Prohibition (1920–1933) had a significant impact on the entire country, its effects on Music Row were particularly notable. As the popularity of this area's live music scene grew, so did the desire for boozy drinks to carry in hand during performances. During Prohibition, the neighborhood had to adapt to the times: speakeasies, known as "blind pigs" or "juice joints," started popping up along the streets, operating discreetly in basements and back rooms, behind unmarked doors, away from public attention. Speakeasy owners were resourceful and creative to ensure they evaded law enforcement, using trapdoors and secret passwords to alert thirsty passersby to the presence of alcohol and to warn of potential raids.

The speakeasies hidden in Music Row were gathering places for musicians, songwriters, and other creatives who met to unwind, collaborate, and imbibe. Here, new sounds were born that furthered the long-lasting artistic spirit of the neighborhood.

THE PATTERSON HOUSE

1711 DIVISION STREET

The Patterson House is a speak-easy-style bar hidden inside a century-old house in Nashville's Midtown, pouring expertly crafted cocktails with a side of Tennessee history just at the end of Music Row. The venue that really introduced the art of craft cocktails to the Music City in 2009, The Patterson House operates with a credo of making drinks with precision, from boutique spirits and seasonal fruit and house-made cordials, bitters, and syrups to a selection of filtered ice cubes chosen specifically with each cocktail in mind.

The name of the Patterson House is a Tennessee Prohibition history lesson in itself. Named after the former governor of The Volunteer State, Malcolm R. Patterson, who in 1909 vetoed the bill that aimed to bring a statewide Prohibition to Tennessee. As Patterson said, "for a State . . . to attempt to control what the people shall eat and drink and wear . . . is tyranny, and not liberty." His efforts, which were overruled at the time by the legislature, are remembered and honored today in this dimly lit speakeasy-style bar where seating is first-come, first-served.

TOMCAT SOUR

PATTERSON HOUSE
1711 DIVISION STREET

This one's a longtime must-order at Midtown's vibey speakeasy-style bar from Strategic Hospitality. Some of the first on the scene to bring Nashville imbibers real-deal cocktail bar experience with consistently well-built drinks, this one from Mark McMinn is a nice place to start on the menu or end a great night out in Nashville from the comfort of your own home bar. This recipe works best with spherical ice.

GLASSWARE: Rocks glass

GARNISH: Mint sprig

- 2 oz. Hayman's Old Tom Gin
- ¾ oz. fresh lemon juice
- ½ oz. Aperol

- ½ oz. Patterson Ginger Syrup (see recipe)
- 5 to 7 mint leaves (not muddled)

1. Combine all of the ingredients in a cocktail shaker and shake.

2. Strain the cocktail into a rocks glass over ice and garnish with a mint sprig.

PATTERSON GINGER SYRUP: In a small saucepan, combine 1 part ginger juice to 1½ parts sugar and heat, stirring constantly until the sugar is dissolved. Allow the syrup to cool.

PRESIDENTIAL SUITE

Upgrade your standard Old Fashioned with this super luxe version of the classic drink, created by Doug Monroe and crafted by the skilled bartenders at Patterson House. A mix of bourbon, rye, and rum, this beverage also includes the satisfying combination of house-made honey syrup and orange bitters. So next time you want to treat yo' self, whip up a round or two of the Presidential Suite—you'll be guaranteed to have a decadent evening.

GLASSWARE: Rocks glass

GARNISH: Orange peel

- 1 oz. Old Forester 100 Proof Bourbon
- 1 oz. Old Overholt Straight Rye Whiskey
- ½ oz. Cruzan Black Strap Rum
- ¼ oz. Honey Syrup (see recipe)
- 2 dashes Angostura orange bitters

1. Combine all of the ingredients in a mixing glass and stir.

2. Strain the cocktail into a rocks glass over ice.

3. Express an orange peel over the drink then garnish with the peel.

HONEY SYRUP: In a small saucepan, combine 3 parts honey to 1 part water and heat, stirring constantly until the ingredients have combined. Allow the syrup to cool.

BLOOD AND SAND

PATTERSON HOUSE
1711 DIVISION STREET

The classic Blood and Sand cocktail originated in the 1920s, named after the 1922 silent film *Blood and Sand*, starring Rudolph Valentino. It gained popularity during the Prohibition era and has since become a beloved classic. Its combination of ingredients represents the four main characters in the film: whiskey for the matador, orange juice for the blood of the bull, cherry liqueur for the love interest, and sweet vermouth representing the sand of the bullring. At Patterson House, Matt Tocco puts his own spin on the classic, and it's just plain delightful.

GLASSWARE: Rocks glass

- 1½ oz. Corsair Triple Smoke American Single Malt Whiskey
- ¾ oz. Punt e Mes
- ¾ oz. Heering Cherry Liqueur
- ¾ oz. fresh lemon juice
- ¾ oz. fresh orange juice
- ⅜ oz. demerara simple syrup

1. Combine all of the ingredients in a cocktail shaker with ice and shake.

2. Strain the cocktail into a rocks glass over a short rectangular prism of ice.

PAPER CHAMPION

Local bar expert Alex McCutchen created this booze-forward Tennessee whiskey–based Patterson House classic—a fan favorite for its bold flavors like apertivo and cardamom bitters.

GLASSWARE: Coupe glass and sidecar

- ¾ oz. Nelson's Green Brier Tennessee Whiskey
- ¾ oz. Dolin Blanc Vermouth
- ¾ oz. Select Aperitivo
- ¾ oz. fresh lemon juice
- ¾ oz. simple syrup
- Dash Angostura orange bitters
- 2 drops Scrappy's Cardamom Bitters
- Lemon peel, to express

1. Combine all of the ingredients, except for the lemon peel, in a cocktail shaker with ice and shake.

2. Strain the cocktail into a coupe.

3. To finish, express a lemon peel over the drink then discard the peel.

GRIFFIN'S DECEPTION

PATTERSON HOUSE
1711 DIVISION STREET

Griffin's Deception "is effectively a smoky, citrusy spin on a White Negroni, named after the main character from the classic Universal monster movie, *The Invisible Man*," says Matt Tuggle, bartender at The Patterson House. "Although the drink is completely clear, the flavor is surprisingly bold and earthy, with a lightly bitter finish. It also highlights the unique flavor of sotol, a spirit which I strongly feel more people should know about."

GLASSWARE: Rocks glass
GARNISH: Grapefruit peel

- 1½ oz. Flor del Desierto Sotol
- ¾ oz. Luxardo Bitter Bianco
- ¾ oz. Dolin Blanc Vermouth
- Dash Scrappy's Grapefruit Bitters

1. Combine all of the ingredients in a mixing glass and stir with ice.

2. Strain the cocktail into a rocks glass over a large ice cube.

3. Garnish with a grapefruit peel.

IT'S ONLY FOREVER

PATTERSON HOUSE
1711 DIVISION STREET

Matt Tuggle describes this drink as one of his favorite-ever creations. It combines the oaky vanilla notes of reposado tequila with drier fruit flavors like apricot and an herbaceous amaro—it's a refreshingly smooth sipper.

GLASSWARE: **Snifter glass**

GARNISH: **Orange peel pigtail**

- 1 oz. reposado tequila
- 1 oz. Cardamaro
- ½ oz. Amaro Meletti
- ½ oz. Giffard Abricot du Roussillon
- Pinch salt

1. Chill a snifter glass. Combine all of the ingredients with ice in a mixing glass and stir.

2. Strain the cocktail into the chilled snifter.

3. Garnish with an orange peel pigtail.

LADY STARDUST

PATTERSON HOUSE
1711 DIVISION STREET

Lady Stardust is a perfect example of what I like to call 'sneaky tiki,' or a drink that somewhat disguises its tropical origins," says Matt Tuggle. "This drink is heavily inspired by the classic Jungle Bird cocktail made with rums, pineapple, lime, and Campari. Lady Stardust takes a more approachable route, using vodka in place of the more potent rum and substituting the smoother Select Aperitivo for the bitterness of Campari. The result is a deliciously fresh and tropical flavor up front, which subtly dries out to a mildly bitter finish."

GLASSWARE: Coupe glass

GARNISH: Thin lime wheel

- 1 blackberry
- 1 raspberry
- 1½ oz. vodka
- 1 oz. fresh pineapple juice
- ¾ oz. Select Aperitivo
- ¾ oz. fresh lime juice
- ½ oz. grenadine
- ¼ oz. vanilla syrup
- 2 dashes Regans' Orange Bitters

1. Chill a coupe glass. Muddle the berries in a shaker tin.

2. Combine the remaining ingredients in the tin with ice and shake vigorously.

3. Strain the cocktail through a fine-mesh strainer into the chilled coupe.

4. Garnish with a thin, floating lime wheel.

A MILLION THINGS TO SAY

PATTERSON HOUSE
1711 DIVISION STREET

his wonderfully refreshing cocktail is like a spa day in a glass," says Matt Tuggle, "combining the cooling flavors of cucumber and coconut with the fresh and vegetal character of cachaça, the popular Brazilian sugarcane spirit. It is surprisingly light, utilizing a blanc vermouth as the base of drink instead of a stronger spirit, which ties together the bolder accenting flavors nicely."

GLASSWARE: Collins glass

GARNISH: Cucumber slice

- **2 slices of cucumber**
- **1½ oz. Dolin Blanc Vermouth**
- **¾ oz. fresh lime juice**
- **¾ oz. cane sugar syrup**
- **½ oz. cachaça**

- **½ oz. Kalani Coconut Liqueur**
- **2 dashes Angostura orange bitters**
- **1 egg white**
- **Splash tonic water**

1. Muddle the cucumber slices in a shaker tin.

2. Combine the remaining ingredients, except for the tonic water, in the tin.

3. Shake vigorously without ice, then add ice and shake again.

4. Pour a splash of tonic water over ice into a collins glass, then strain the cocktail into the same glass.

5. Garnish with a slice of cucumber.

THE GREAT BAMBINO

Not your everyday riff on a Negroni, The Pool Club combines Kahlúa, Carpano Antica Formula Vermouth, and reposado tequila, with Amaro Montenegro doing the work in balancing it all out for a refreshing poolside sip with a view. The bonus? Seeing the queen Dolly Parton herself at the bottom of your glass.

GLASSWARE: **Rocks glass**

GARNISH: **Lemon swath**

- **1 oz. Amaro Montenegro**
- **1 oz. Carpano Antica Formula Vermouth**
- **1 oz. Kahlúa**
- **½ oz. reposado tequila**

1. Combine all of the ingredients in a mixing glass with ice and stir.

2. Strain the cocktail over a large cube into a rocks glass.

3. Garnish with a lemon swath.

WEDGEWOOD-HOUSTON/
GERMANTOWN

GOODTIMES GIMLET

HANDSOME JOHNNY

STEVE MCQUEEN

CUMBERLAND COOLER

CHILI LEMON

MELON KUSH

GOOD TIME LEMON DROP

Wedgewood-Houston is a not-so-hidden Nashville gem, with an industrial past and Civil War ties, that today is brimming with a fiercely independent spirit and copious amounts of coffee and cocktail destinations. The neighborhood that sent socks to the moon (yep, the socks Neil Armstrong and Buzz Aldrin wore on the moon came from the old May Hosiery factory at Chestnut and Houston) today is home to Nashville's first soccer stadium, an exclusive artists-only social club, with much more to come as one of the most quickly developing parts of town.

Germantown, one of the city's oldest suburbs, boasts stunning, quaint nineteenth-century architecture. Despite their distinct identities, these communities are united by a shared Nashville spirit, a testament to the city's diverse yet harmonious character.

GOODTIMES GIMLET

GOODTIMES
1529 4TH AVENUE SOUTH

T he gimlet has long been a staple in the cocktail community. It's believed to be dated back to the nineteenth century when British Navy soldiers would drink it to ward off scurvy. "At GoodTimes," says Jamie White, "we take a fun, modern approach to the simple classic, adding yuzu and rosemary."

GLASSWARE: Coupe glass

GARNISH: Rosemary sprig, lime wheel

- 1½ oz. Fords London Dry Gin
- ¾ oz. Rosemary Syrup (see recipe)
- ½ oz. yuzu juice
- ¼ oz. St-Germain Elderflower Liqueur

1. Chill a coupe glass. Shake all of the ingredients together with ice in a cocktail shaker.

2. Fine-strain the cocktail into the chilled coupe.

3. Garnish with a rosemary sprig and a lime wheel.

ROSEMARY SYRUP: In a small saucepan over medium heat, combine 1 cup water, 1 cup sugar, and 4 sprigs of rosemary. Cook until the sugar dissolves then turn off the heat and allow the syrup to cool. Strain the syrup.

HANDSOME JOHNNY

LUCKY'S 3 STAR BAR
1401 4TH AVENUE SOUTH

John Prine lived in Nashville for the later years in his life, says Jamie White. "He frequented local dive bars. His favorite drink was a vodka and ginger ale with a lime. He said if he ever got to name this drink, he would call it a 'Handsome Johnny.' When he passed in 2020, we decided to make that drink a staple on our highball menu at Lucky's 3 Star. This is a super easy one to make at home!"

GLASSWARE: Highball glass

GARNISH: Lime wedge

- 2 oz. vodka
- ¼ oz. fresh lime juice
- Ginger ale, to top

1. In a highball glass filled with ice, combine the vodka and lime juice.

2. Top with ginger ale and garnish with a lime wedge.

STEVE MCQUEEN

EARNEST BAR & HIDEAWAY
438 HOUSTON STREET #160

The antihero of your father's Manhattan, this is the flagship cocktail of Earnest Bar & Hideaway. It has won a whopping twelve different awards and is the legacy cocktail of owner and veteran bar expert Christopher Weber.

GLASSWARE: Rocks glass

GARNISH: Flamed orange peel

- 2 oz. rye whiskey
- ½ oz. Amaro Averna
- ½ oz. Amaro Meletti
- 4 dashes old-fashioned bitters

1. Build the cocktail in a mixing glass over ice.

2. Stir for 15 seconds for dilution.

3. Strain the cocktail over fresh ice into a rocks glass.

4. Garnish with a flamed orange peel.

CUMBERLAND COOLER

GERMANTOWN PUB
708 MONROE STREET

A quintessential summer pastime of choice in Music City is gathering friends for a relaxing canoe float down the Cumberland River. It's a great way to enjoy the weather, the views, and, if you've prepared, this refreshing cocktail. Easy to pre-batch for pool parties or day trips, this mélange of cooling flavors will have you feeling like you're out for a lazy float.

GLASSWARE: Collins glass

- 1 oz. Conniption American Dry Gin
- ½ oz. St-Germain Elderflower Liqueur
- ½ oz. fresh lime juice
- ¼ oz. simple syrup
- Diced cucumbers, to taste

1. Combine all of the ingredients, except for the cucumbers, in a cocktail tin.

2. Add the diced cucumbers, shake, and strain the cocktail over ice into a collins glass.

CHILI LEMON

GERMANTOWN PUB
708 MONROE STREET

Life is about balance, *right*? Sweet and spicy, work and play, fight and make up? This cocktail has you covered from the crisp acidity of lemon and lime, tingling spice of Tajín, deep golden sweetness of agave, a clean kick from fresh jalapeños, and the showpiece: Bacardí Mango Chile Rum. There's something for everyone, but as SNL's Chris Kattan once said, "Can you handle the Mango?"

GLASSWARE: **Collins glass**

GARNISH: **Lime wedge, 3 jalapeño slices**

- Tajín, for the rim
- 2 oz. Bacardí Mango Chile Rum
- 1 oz. fresh lemon juice
- 1 oz. agave nectar
- 2 fresh jalapeño slices

1. Wet the rim of half of a collins glass with a lime wedge then dip the glass half in Tajín seasoning.

2. In a cocktail shaker with ice, combine all of the ingredients and shake.

3. Strain the cocktail over ice into the collins glass and garnish with a lime wedge.

MELON KUSH

GERMANTOWN PUB
708 MONROE STREET

H emp or hempseed vodka is a relatively new trend on the spirits scene. It's a sustainable alternative to existing vodka production techniques and often has a unique flavor profile of light nuttiness and earthiness. These characteristics blend well with notes of melon and pineapple to create a lush, fruit-forward experience that will leave your mood elevated.

✳

GLASSWARE: 12 oz. glass

- 1½ oz. hempseed vodka
- 1 oz. pineapple juice
- ½ oz. melon liqueur
- ½ oz. fresh lemon juice
- ½ oz. simple syrup

1. Combine all of the ingredients in a shaker and shake.

2. Pour the cocktail over ice into a 12 oz. glass.

GOOD TIME LEMON DROP

GERMANTOWN PUB
708 MONROE STREET

T ry a THC-infused liqueur in this take on a Lemon Drop for an extra level. Is that an oompaloompa? Enjoy responsibly.

GLASSWARE: Rocks or martini glass

- **Sugar, for the rim (optional)**
- **1½ oz. Western Son Blueberry Vodka**
- **½ oz. triple sec**
- **1 oz. nonalcoholic THC-infused liqueur**

1. Wet the rim of a rocks or martini glass with water then dip the glass in sugar, if desired.

2. Combine all of the ingredients in a mixing glass.

3. Pour the cocktail over ice into the glass.

TENNESSEE WHISKEY

HONEY I'M HOME

THE WISE SAGE

8 TO THE PUNCH

GOO-GOOD PUNCH

JIMMY'S HORSE NECK

LYNCHBURG LEMONADE

SUMMER IN SCENIC CITY

A book about Nashville cocktails would be as dry as five of Tennessee's counties without a chapter dedicated to the spirit that put the Volunteer State on the map as a drinking destination. Today, there's even a Tennessee Whiskey Trail. What sets Tennessee whiskey apart is the additional step of charcoal filtering, known as the Lincoln County Process.

The Lincoln County Process involves dripping the newly distilled whiskey through charcoal made from sugar maple wood before aging the whiskey in barrels. This filtration is believed to impart a smoother and mellower flavor to the whiskey.

In terms of legal definitions, the state of Tennessee has specific requirements for a whiskey to be labeled as "Tennessee whiskey:" 1) it must be produced within the state, and 2) it must undergo the Lincoln County Process.

The best-known Tennessee whiskey is Jack Daniel's, founded by Jasper Newton "Jack" Daniel in 1866 and now renowned worldwide.

Paradoxically, Jack Daniel's Distillery is located in a dry county. For many years, that meant completely dry, but today Moore County allows the sale of commemorative bottles of Jack in the White Rabbit Bottle Shop, and one can take part in a sampling tour at the distillery. It is also now possible to sample wine, rum, vodka, and whiskey in shops where it is distilled on premises. Beer is also available in local food establishments when served with a meal now in Moore County.

NATHAN "NEAREST" GREEN

Of course, Jack Daniel's claims the title of one of America's most iconic whiskey brands, but the man who started it all was actually Nathan "Nearest" Green, an enslaved African American who taught young Jack Daniel the art of whiskey distillation.

Born in Maryland in 1820, it's not clear where or how Green arrived in Lincoln County, Tennessee. But by the mid-1800s, he was such a skilled distiller that his enslavers, the Landis & Green Company, would rent him out to local farms and plantations who hoped to benefit from his whiskey-making expertise, and it's said that during one of these events is where Green met a young Jasper "Jack" Daniel, a 7-year-old orphan who was looking for work and to escape a rough home life. Daniel wound up on the property of a Lynchburg preacher, Dan Call, who was also a distiller. (Previously, it was Dan Call who was credited with teaching young Jack Daniel to make whiskey.)

Despite the odds, Green's story emerged from the shadows of history, underlining the profound influence of his craftsmanship in the whiskey industry. Nearest Green was actually credited as the first master distiller for the now-famous Jack Daniel's Tennessee Whiskey (Jack Daniel himself being the second). Green was the one who taught Daniel the sugar maple charcoal filtering, today recognized as the Lincoln County Process.

Researchers have gone on to discover that many enslaved people played much larger roles than previously thought in America's early whiskey-making. For example, famous plantation owners including presidents Andrew Jackson and George Washington were said to have used enslaved workers to run their distilleries. According to spirits writer Fred Minnick, author of *Bourbon: The Rise, Fall, and Rebirth of an American Whiskey*, at auctions of enslaved people, some brokers would "notate distiller-trained slaves, many of whom previously worked on Caribbean sugarcane plantations and contributed to the distillation of sugar's byproduct, molasses, to create rum. These skill sets earned premiums for their owners and made them attractive to buyers." Specific documentation of enslaved people's ties to whiskey, and Tennessee whiskey, however, remain hard to find, as credit was not given where it was due.

HUMBLE BARON AT NEAREST GREEN DISTILLERY

3125 US-231, SHELBYVILLE

The Guinness Book of World Records' official "World's Longest Bar" is located just a short drive southeast of Nashville. At Nearest Green Distillery, in Shelbyville, Humble Baron's showpiece bar is a whopping 518 feet long, featuring 17 stations, wrapped around an indoor stage.

The bar program was crafted in partnership with Gin & Luck, the hospitality company behind renowned cocktail institution Death & Co., with Black-owned spirits taking center stage. Beverage director DeAndre A. Jackson leads the bar's cocktail innovation, with Espresso Martinis, Old Fashioneds, Juleps, and even Mimosas made with their own Uncle Nearest 1856 Premium Aged Whiskey.

When it comes to entertainment, Humble Baron pulls out all the stops. The audio and visual setup for the state-of-the-art music venue is a work of art, meticulously designed by the former technical director and engineer of Prince's legendary Paisley Park. With both indoor and outdoor stages, the venue is primed to accommodate over 15,000 guests for a mind-blowing live music experience.

HONEY I'M HOME

HUMBLE BARON AT NEAREST GREEN DISTILLERY
3125 US-231, SHELBYVILLE

To create this sweet and spicy cocktail, DeAndre Jackson uses a Nashville-inspired hot honey syrup that the team makes in-house. The flavor inspiration comes from the Nashville hot chicken dish, replicating the spicy kick with a surprising hint of heat as the hot honey hits the back of your palate.

GLASSWARE: Double old-fashioned glass

GARNISH: Dehydrated lemon wheel

- 1 oz. Uncle Nearest 1856 Premium Aged Whiskey
- 1 oz. Equiano Original Rum
- ¾ oz. fresh pineapple juice
- ½ oz. fresh lemon juice
- ½ oz. Hot Honey Syrup (see recipe)

1. Combine all of the ingredients in a cocktail shaker with ice and shake.

2. Strain the cocktail into a double old-fashioned glass and garnish with a dehydrated lemon wheel.

HOT HONEY SYRUP: In a small container, combine 2 parts Mike's Hot Honey and 1 part warm water and stir until well combined. Bottle and store in the refrigerator.

AKINDE OLAGUNDOYE, HUMBLE BARON AT NEAREST GREEN DISTILLERY

A Nashville resident since 2016, Akinde Olagundoye was born and raised in Brooklyn by his Panamanian mother and Nigerian father. He attended Oakwood University in Huntsville, Alabama, where he found his passion for service, bartending, and cocktails. And ever since he joined the United States Bartenders' Guild (USBG), he has been practicing, learning, teaching, and spreading the gospel of great cocktails. Akinde is the vice president of the Nashville chapter of the USBG and bar manager at Humble Baron, the world's longest bar, located at Nearest Green Distillery in Shelbyville.

When he's not crafting drinks at Humble Baron, Akinde is the bar lead at AB Hillsboro Village and brand ambassador for Filthy Food, a premium cocktail mixer and garnish company based in Miami.

What did you want to be when you grew up?

A medical doctor. Pediatrician, to be specific.

What drew you to Humble Baron?

I've always been a huge fan of whiskey. Living in Nashville, I became an even bigger fan of Tennessee whiskey. I was drawn to Uncle Nearest from its inception. Uncle Nearest is a premium Tennessee whiskey founded on the history of Nathan "Nearest" Green. He was a Black man who taught Jasper "Jack Daniel" Newton how to make whiskey, using the Lincoln County Process of sugar maple charcoal filtration. When I heard that "the longest bar in the world" was opening at Nearest Green Distillery, I imme-diately knew I had to be a part of it.

In a field where people move around a lot, what makes you stay with this bar program?

We opened Humble Baron on March 23, 2023, so it's only been five months, but I feel at home there. The owners, Keith and Fawn Weaver, treat us like family. Our team is diverse in every aspect. Being there from the start has given me an opportunity to help bring it all together as one cohesive unit, and shape the direction in which it will grow. It is challeng-ing, and therefore more rewarding. We are in the Guinness Book of World Records, and we are just getting started. One of my favorite perks is get-ting to be around horses. The property is beautiful. The sky's the limit.

What's your go-to cocktail order?

My go-to cocktail order is an Uncle Nearest Rye Vieux Carré. It's a classic cocktail that originated in New Orleans at the Hotel Monteleone. It has the perfect balance of strong rye whiskey and soft cognac, along with rais-iny, honeyed sweetness, herbs, spice, bitterness, and citrus.

What is your favorite "bartenders hang" bar?

My favorite industry bar in town would have to be Mickey's Tavern. It's in the neighborhood and it's chill enough for an after-work beverage.

Where else would you send a visiting tourist to drink in Nashville?

I really enjoy going to The Fox Bar & Cocktail Club, Rosemary and the Beauty Queen, Mother's Ruin, And Skull's Rainbow Room, to name a few.

What are must-have things to have on hand for someone's bar at home?

Every home bar needs a quality cocktail shaker tin set for shaken drinks, a barspoon for stirred ones, a jigger for measuring, and plenty of ice. You can use fancy molds or get it straight out of an ice tray, but you cannot forget the ice. After that, I would stock my favorite spirits and mixers, fol-lowed by a few other options to share with friends.

THE WISE SAGE

HUMBLE BARON AT NEAREST GREEN DISTILLERY
3125 US-231, SHELBYVILLE

With the premium whiskey and the dance of flavors—sage, lemon, bitters, and more—this complex cocktail is a rewarding one to prepare.

GLASSWARE: Rocks glass

GARNISH: Lemon peel, sage leaves

- 1½ oz. Uncle Nearest 1856 Premium Aged Whiskey
- ½ oz. Kronan Swedish Punsch
- ¼ oz. Vanilla Sage Syrup (see recipe)
- 2 dashes Bitter Queens Marie Laveau Tobacco Bitters

1. Add all of the ingredients to a mixing glass with ice and stir until well chilled.

2. Strain the cocktail into a rocks glass over a large rock or fresh ice cubes.

3. Express a lemon peel over the cocktail then add the peel as garnish, along with sage leaves.

VANILLA SAGE SYRUP: In a small saucepan over medium heat, combine 1 cup sugar and 1 cup water and stir until the sugar is dissolved. Remove the simple syrup from heat and add 1 vanilla bean, split lengthwise, and 6 to 8 fresh, whole sage leaves. Let the syrup steep for at least 2 hours before straining it into a jar. Allow it to cool completely before using.

8 TO THE BAR

Cynar's artichoke notes and the uplift of fresh basil give this silky smooth gin-based cocktail a bright, refreshing nose.

GLASSWARE: Rocks glass

GARNISH: 1 basil leaf, lemon peel

- 1½ oz. Tanqueray N° Ten Gin
- ¾ oz. St-Germain Elderflower Liqueur
- ½ oz. Cynar
- 4 basil leaves

1. Add all of the ingredients to a mixing glass with ice and stir until well chilled.

2. Strain the cocktail into a rocks glass over a large rock or fresh ice cubes.

3. Garnish with a basil leaf and express a lemon peel over the cocktail, then add the peel as garnish.

LIQUOR LAB

144 2ND AVENUE NORTH SUITE 10

If you're in Nashville and looking to hone your mixology skills to the next level, grab your boots and a bestie and sign up for an immersive mixology experience at Liquor Lab.

Nashville represents the second location for New York–based Liquor Lab, and the Music City outpost sits right on Second Avenue, steps away from the hustle and bustle of Lower Broadway, but with an entirely different drinking experience altogether. There's no honky-tonk music or party buses to distract here, and the expert bartenders who serve as instructors in Liquor Lab's underground classrooms are fully focused on guiding attendees throughout the process of crafting a perfect cocktail.

Whether you're a connoisseur or a complete novice, there's a lesson for everyone, including trade secrets from the pro mixologists. Of course, the Art of the Old Fashioned and Bourbon & Beyond classes are especially appealing to whiskey aficionados, while others flock to classes dedicated specifically to other classics like Espresso Martinis, Margaritas, zero-proof drinks, and more.

GOO-GOOD PUNCH

This cocktail is Liquor Lab's nod to Nashville's iconic candy—the Goo Goo Cluster, still made today using the original recipe from 1912. The circular mound of caramel, marshmallow nougat, fresh roasted peanuts, and real milk chocolate was the first candy bar to have its shape, which made it more difficult to package than the conventional regular- and square-shape candy bars of its time. Visits to the Nashville chocolate factory where these treats are made include classes and tours. You can also place orders online for shipping.

GLASSWARE: Double old-fashioned glass

GARNISH: Dehydrated lemon wheel

- 2 oz. peanut butter–washed Tennessee whiskey
- 3 dashes bitters
- ½ oz. marshmallow chocolate milk cordial

1. Add all of the ingredients to a double old-fashioned glass over one large ice cube.

2. Stir, then garnish with a dehydrated lemon wheel.

JIMMY'S HORSE NECK

LIQUOR LAB
144 2ND AVENUE NORTH SUITE 10

Many Nashvillians first learned about the heirloom Jimmy Red Corn when Nashville-based celebrity chef Sean Brock first brought it to their attention—but for nearly a century, Jimmy Red Corn was used by bootleggers to make their moonshine whiskey. The variety was near extinction early in the 2000s, but a duo of remaining ears of corn were used to revive it. Today, it's a coveted ingredient throughout Nashville and the South as a whole, prized by both chefs and distillers alike.

GLASSWARE: Collins glass

GARNISH: Orange peel

- Chili salt, for the rim
- 2 oz. Tennessee whiskey
- Dash orange bitters
- 1 oz. Jimmy Red Corn Cordial (see recipe)
- Soda water, to top

1. Wet the rim of a collins glass with an orange slice then dip the glass in chili salt. Pack the glass with ice.

2. In the glass, combine all of the ingredients, except for the soda water, and stir until the glass is ice cold.

3. Top with soda water. Garnish with an orange peel.

JIMMY RED CORN CORDIAL: Remove the kernels from 4 to 5 ears of Jimmy Red Corn (3 cups of kernels). Blend the corn with water then strain the mixture to collect the juice. Combine the corn juice and 3 cups sugar in a saucepan and simmer for 5 minutes on medium heat. Allow the mixture to cool to room temperature, then stir in 40 grams citric acid and a pinch salt. Transfer the cordial to a bottle and store in the refrigerator for up to 2 weeks.

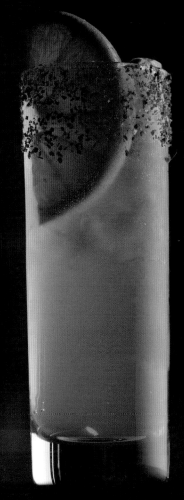

LYNCHBURG LEMONADE

J ack Daniel's is famously distilled in a dry county in Tennessee. Although Lynchburg Lemonade is named after the world-famous whiskey's hometown, the porch-sippin' cocktail was actually created just south, in Huntsville, Alabama, in 1980 by bar owner and musician Tony Mason. Mason sued the distillery for promoting (without giving him credit) the drink he created, but the judge only awarded him $1. The case was retried later and the distillery won again, this time arguing that the recipe wasn't even a trade secret. Maybe it's not, but the result is fizzy and refreshing, nonetheless.

GLASSWARE: **Collins or hurricane glass**

GARNISH: **Lemon slices**

- 1½ oz. Jack Daniel's Old No. 7
- 1½ oz. sweet-and-sour mix
- 1½ oz. triple sec
- Lemon-lime soda, chilled, to top

1. Fill a collins or hurricane glass with ice.

2. Add the whiskey, sweet-and-sour mix, and triple sec and mix with a tall spoon.

3. Top with chilled soda and garnish with lemon slices.

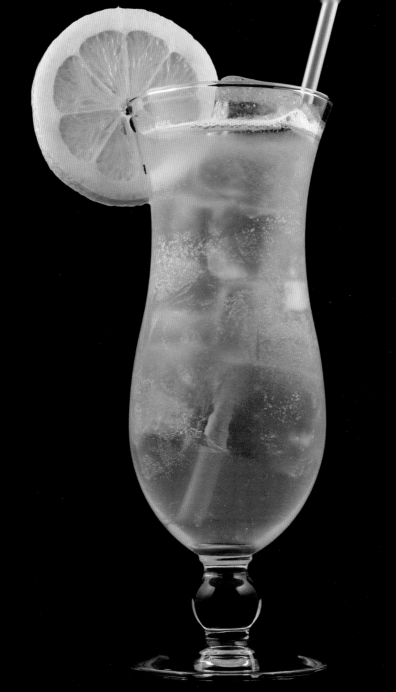

SUMMER IN SCENIC CITY

CHATTANOOGA WHISKEY
1439 MARKET STREET, CHATTANOOGA

This cocktail from Chattanooga Whiskey's Sara Serkownek is an ideal summer sipper built around their award-winning Chattanooga Whiskey 91, which has notes of butterscotch pudding, dried apricot, honeyed toast, and pound cake.

GLASSWARE: Coupe glass
GARNISH: Lemon twist

- 6 raspberries
- 1½ oz. Chattanooga Whiskey 91
- ½ oz. orgeat
- ¾ oz. fresh lemon juice

1. Gently muddle the raspberries in a shaking tin.

2. Add ice, the whiskey, orgeat, and lemon juice, and shake until well chilled.

3. Fine-strain the cocktail into a coupe.

4. Garnish with a lemon twist.

NASHVILLE-AREA TENNESSEE WHISKEY DISTILLERIES

If you're down for a Vol State brown water crawl, you can get a passport for the Tennessee Whiskey Trail, which has over twenty-five prime spots for a whiskey experience, but here are a few close-to-Nashville spots to check out. If you get all your passport pages stamped, you'll get a gift for your dedication to the cause. (Grab a digital passport at www.tnwhiskeytrail.com.)

CORSAIR DISTILLERY
601 MERRITT AVENUE

Originally founded in Kentucky in 2008, they made their move to Nashville in 2010 and became Tennessee's first new legal craft distillery since Prohibition. And it's no surprise that their unique lineup of spirits has earned them over 800 national and international awards since. From their whiskey and rye to their more unusual small-batch spirits, each creation carries a touch of innovation, a splash of boldness, and a generous serving of quality. Everything is made in-house using a pre–Prohibition Era still, giving each spirit a unique taste that cannot be found anywhere else. Be sure and try *Whisky Advocate*'s chosen Artisan Whiskey of the Year and the one that put Corsair on the map: the Corsair Triple Smoke, featuring three individual smoked malts (cherrywood from Wisconsin, beechwood from Germany, and peat from Scotland).

Standard Proof Whiskey Co. (see page 172)

LEIPER'S FORK DISTILLERY
3381 SOUTHALL ROAD, FRANKLIN

Nestled in Nashville's scenic countryside in a 200-year-old log cabin in Leiper's Fork, Lee Kennedy's distillery takes tradition seriously. An undeniable gem for whiskey connoisseurs and curious visitors alike, this distillery is a testament to traditional craftsmanship, where each batch of whiskey is meticulously produced using locally harvested grains. A tour of their facility offers a fascinating glimpse into the distilling process, from grain to glass, narrated with a blend of wit, wisdom, and a deep respect for the craft. Be sure and try their TN Whiskey Bottled in Bond—it's beautifully balanced, made using not only rye, but also toasted malted barley. Caramel and spice make this an easy drinker by the fire or on a heated outdoor patio.

NASHVILLE CRAFT DISTILLERY
514 HAGAN STREET

What happens when a scientist gets his hands on grains and botanicals? It all marries to create an intoxicating blend of science and artistry. With a focus on local and regional ingredients, Wedgewood-Houston's Nashville Craft Distillery was born of a scientist's mind, with former DNA laboratory director Bruce Boeko opening the distillery in March of 2016. They produce whiskey, gin, sorghum spirits, and other craft spirits.

NELSON'S GREEN BRIER DISTILLERY
1414 CLINTON STREET

History and family heritage lay at the heart of Nelson's Green Brier Distillery in Nashville. Brothers Andy and Charlie Nelson resurrected their family whiskey business a couple decades back, paying homage to their roots before the days of Prohibition in Greenbrier, Tennessee. While whiskey drinkers are sometimes wary of historical legacies and stories, this one has legs, as their great-, great-, great-grandfather, Charles Nelson, was producing nearly fifteen times as much whiskey as Jack Daniel's was in the 1880s. Furthering their Tennessee whiskey street cred, Nelson's original distillery was shuttered by state Prohibition in 1909 and is now a registered historical site.

STANDARD PROOF WHISKEY CO.
219 REP. JOHN LEWIS WAY NORTH

Truly born behind the bar in Nashville, Standard Proof Whiskey Co. offers an imaginative lineup of creative director Robert Longhurst's craft rye whiskey that was originally a well-kept secret shared only among fellow bartenders and regular patrons. Standard Proof's first signature whiskey infusion was a coffee expression called Red Eye Rye—it launched in 2017 and catapulted the brand as a leader.

PENNINGTON DISTILLING CO.
900 44TH AVENUE NORTH

Established in 2011, Pennington Distilling Co. is located in Nashville's Nations neighborhood. The grain-to-glass independent distillery has aged and clear spirits along with other products. Their current small-batch spirit roster includes Davidson Reserve Whiskey, Pickers Vodka, the award-winning Whisper Creek Tennessee Sipping Cream, and Walton's Finest Vodka. The Davidson Reserve Tennessee Whiskey, with notes of caramel and toasted marshmallows, was the first locally distilled, small-batch Tennessee whiskey.

TENNESSEE WHISKEY PLAYLIST

The now famous spirit-centered love song, "Tennessee Whiskey," was written in 1981 by Dean Dillon and Linda Hargrove, who decided to hang out and write a song together after meeting at Nashville's historic Bluebird Cafe. Dean had toyed with the idea for it for some time, so the story goes that they went back to Hargrove's house and wrote the song at 4 o'clock in the morning, in true Nashville fashion. After its completion, the song was first offered to George Strait, but he turned it down. "Tennessee Whiskey" was first recorded by David Allan Coe for his 1981 album of the same name, and then by George Jones, who took it to number 2 on the country chart in 1983. Chris Stapleton's version was certified six-times multiplatinum and by early 2020 was approaching 2 million digital sales.

"Tennessee Whiskey"	Chris Stapleton
"Tennessee Whiskey"	George Jones
"Tennessee Whiskey"	David Allan Coe
"5 Shots of Whiskey"	Hank Williams III
"The Letter That Johnny Walker Red"	Asleep at the Wheel
"Whiskey Girl"	Toby Keith
"Whiskey Lullaby"	Brad Paisley and Alison Krauss
"Jack Daniel's"	Miranda Lambert
"Whiskey"	Jana Kramer
"Whiskey Glasses"	Morgan Wallen
"Cheap Whiskey"	Martina McBride
"Whiskey and You"	Chris Stapleton
"Whiskey, Whiskey"	Kris Kristofferson
"The Whiskey Ain't Workin'"	Travis Tritt
"Whiskey's Gone"	Zac Brown Band
"Whiskey River"	Willie Nelson

Miranda Lambert

Chris Stapleton

Morgan Wallen

ZERO PROOF: NASHVILLE'S THRIVING NONALCOHOLIC (NA) COCKTAILS MOVEMENT

NO FUN AT ALL, AKA THE KILLJOY

NIGHT MOVES

PATRICE

ROSANNA

EYES ADJUST

APERITIVO FIZZ

MORIR SOÑANDO

WITBIER SHANDY

Nashville might be best known as a "drinking town with a music problem," but what's super exciting for those who don't drink, or those taking a night, week, or month off booze, is the city's thriving nonalcoholic (NA) movement. More and more locals and visitors are exploring the city's burgeoning NA scene, proving that you don't need a high-proof cocktail to enjoy a night out. From sober pop-up bars offering innovative NA concoctions and restaurants creating their own zero-proof pairings for their culinary masterpieces to Nashville's first NA bottle shop, Nashville is redefining the zero-proof cocktail experience.

This movement is not just about the drinks, but about the rich social connections and shared experiences that highlight the city's fun and inclusive spirit. In Nashville, everyone's invited to the party, whether they're toasting with a bourbon, THC-infused liqueur, or a beetroot zero-proof cocktail. Check websites like A Fresh Sip (afreshsip.com) for the harder-to-come-by spirits.

STEPHANIE STYLL, KILLJOY

2020 LINDELL AVENUE

When Stephanie Styll opened Killjoy, Nashville's only specialty beverage shop, in early 2023, she had a dream in mind of uniting people and normalizing having a good time without alcohol.

What made you decide to open Killjoy?

I saw alcohol-free (AF) bottle shops opening in big cities and wished Nashville had one. With the growing market, I decided Nashville was ready, and just went for it. The NA scene in Nashville is truly having its moment.

What is the coolest thing about being a part of this growing movement in Nashville?

Building community and being a part of changing the culture. People are seeking out AF options for many reasons—health, curiosity, wellness, pregnancy, and recovery—and our shop is a nexus for it all. You no longer have to identify as an alcoholic to choose AF drink options. We host alcohol-free events and workshops bringing people together in a way that normalizes having a good time and drinking fabulous drinks with nary a drop of alcohol in sight. This is how you change the culture!

What are some trends you see in the NA scene?

Brand-new beverages. People are creating complex adult beverages like nothing you've ever tasted before, and they are SO fun! Yes, it's nice to be able to have a zero-proof G & T or Margarita, but new flavors, textures, and functions are on the horizon. It's honestly about to get way more interesting than the traditional alcohol market because the options are so creative and wide ranging. There is also a real emergence of functional beverages: people want what they drink to actually improve their well-being over time, and contain adaptogens and nootropics, which are wonderful.

What's your go-to zero-proof drink of choice?

Sparkling rosé—delicious, beautiful, low-cal, goes with everything.

Any recommendations for those looking to explore a life sans alcohol?

Mindset is everything! I believe life is more fun post-alcohol because I see examples of it every day. I see the color, brightness, and joy return to people after they give up booze. I hear their stories, and it's also been true in my own life. Surround yourself with encouragement and always have a tasty AF drink in your hand so that you don't feel left out. The old narratives that you have to hit rock bottom to quit or that life will be boring and sanitized are simply not real.

What are some of your favorite brands that you carry at Killjoy?

For beer, I love our local brewery, Southern Grist. Their Company Pilsner is my favorite of all AF beers. For wines, I'm a big fan of Noughty and Leitz. Anything from either of those lines will not disappoint. For spirits, I like NKD LDY and Amethyst, as well as functional brands like 3 Spirit and Dromme. For ready-to-drinks (RTDs), For Bitter or Worse and Parch are amazing, and I love Hiyos. For mixers, you can't go wrong with local Nashville legend Perfectly Cordial. They make a variety of delicious flavors.

Favorite moment since opening Killjoy?

Chris Marshall from Sans Bar singing "Man! I Feel Like a Woman!" [the Shania Twain song] on karaoke. He knows how to get a party going! He's also been a sober celebrity I've been following for years, so having him throw a party in our space was a real "pinch me" moment! Being featured as one of the top US bottle shops in *Wine Enthusiast* didn't suck either.

How does the NA movement impact Nashville as a whole?

Nashville is a drinking town, but it's also a creative town, and I think more and more people are realizing that alcohol holds them back from realizing their full potential. As that happens, I think we'll see more people join this movement and help keep Nashville the thriving creative and musical place it always has been. Look around: many of our top chefs, musicians, and influencers are already publicly alcohol-free. I am grateful to them for leading the way and hope many others will follow. I think Nashville will keep the party going just as strong, but many of us will have something new and fabulous AF in our glasses.

NO FUN AT ALL, AKA THE KILLJOY

KILLJOY BOOZE-FREE BEVERAGE SHOP
2020 LINDELL AVENUE

I f you've never tried a zero-proof tequila, the flavor similarities to regular tequila are pretty fascinating. Bare Zero's Zero Proof Reposado Style Tequila hits all the right notes of agave, with hints of serrano and fresh-cut grass. Stephanie Styll pairs it with a great Nashville restaurant's own house-made tonic, which is available for retail purchase at the Iberian-inspired restaurant. For the tonic water, you can also use Franklin & Sons Premium Indian Tonic Water.

GLASSWARE: Collins glass

GARNISH: Grapefruit peel

- 2 parts Bare Zero Proof Reposado Style Tequila
- Dash simple syrup
- 1 part Peninsula Savory Tonic, to top

1. Combine the NA tequila and simple syrup in a cocktail shaker with ice and shake.

2. Pour the cocktail into a collins glass over ice and top with the tonic water.

3. Express a grapefruit peel over the drink then add the peel as garnish.

NIGHT MOVES

This drink was inspired by The Fox Bar & Cocktail Club's Batteries Not Included. Stephanie Styll's spin relies on the incredible NA amaro The Pathfinder Hemp & Root and cold brew from Killjoy's neighboring coffee shop, The Loading Dock, but feel to use your local cold brew of choice.

GLASSWARE: Coupe glass
GARNISH: Cold foam, orange slice (optional)

- **2 oz. cold brew coffee**
- **1 oz. The Pathfinder Hemp and Root**

- **2 oz. Untitled Art Chocolate Milk Dark Brew**

1. Mix the cold brew and NA liqueur in a cocktail shaker with ice and shake vigorously.

2. Stir in the chocolate milk stout, then strain the mocktail into a coupe.

3. Garnish with cold foam and an orange slice, if desired.

PATRICE

The nonalcoholic trend finally has its moment in Nashville, and Hathorne's beverage director Hayley Teague invites non-drinkers to come back time and again for her zero-proof concoctions. Designed with the Spritz in mind, this one starts with Proxies Pastiche as the base, adding a lovely house-made citrus herbal syrup and a pleasant pop from sparkling mineral water.

GLASSWARE: Wineglass

GARNISH: Fresh herbs, edible flowers

- **4 oz. Proxies Pastiche**
- **1 oz. Citrus & Herb Syrup (see recipe)**
- **3 to 4 oz. club soda, to top**

1. Combine the nonalcoholic wine and the syrup in a cocktail shaker with ice and shake.

2. Strain the cocktail over fresh ice into a wineglass.

3. Top with soda.

4. Garnish with fresh herbs and edible flowers.

CITRUS & HERB SYRUP: In a saucepan, combine 1 sliced lemon, 1 sliced orange, 1 cup water, 1 cup cane sugar, and a mix of aromatic herbs (use any combination of thyme, bay leaf, rosemary, and anise hyssop) and heat the mixture until the sugar is dissolved and the herbs have infused the solution. Allow the syrup to reach room temperature. Strain, bottle, and refrigerate it.

ROSANNA

HATHORNE
4708 CHARLOTTE AVENUE

S piritless Jalisco 55 is the star of yet another of Hayley Teague's fabulous zero-proof creations at Hathorne. This herbaceous reposado-style faux spirit has hints of honey, spicy oak, vanilla, and a delicate peppery kick to finish.

GLASSWARE: Collins glass

GARNISH: Jalapeño slice, mint sprig

- 1½ oz. Jalisco 55 Non-Alcoholic Tequila
- 1 oz. fresh lime juice
- 1 dropper Saline Solution (see recipe on page 268)
- ¾ oz. Monin Strawberry Syrup
- 1 to 2 jalapeño slices

1. Combine all of the ingredients in a cocktail shaker with ice and shake.

2. Dump the contents of the shaker into a collins glass.

3. Garnish with a jalapeño slice and a fresh mint sprig.

EYES ADJUST

HUSK
37 RUTLEDGE STREET

When creating this sober-friendly beverage, Husk's bar manager Adam Morgan wanted to introduce something that could be sipped slowly, like a Martini. The vermouth adds nice tea-like tannins, the verjus adds bright acidity, and the watermelon rounds it all out with texture and subtle sweetness.

GLASSWARE: Rocks glass

GARNISH: Shiso leaf

- **2½ oz. Martini Non-Alcoholic Floreale**
- **¾ oz. blanc verjus**
- **½ oz. Watermelon-Shiso Syrup (see recipe)**
- **Pinch sea salt**
- **Lime peel**

1. Combine all of the ingredients, except for the lime peel, in a mixing glass and stir over ice for 20 seconds.

2. Strain the mocktail over a large ice cube into a rocks glass.

3. Express a lime peel over the cocktail, then add the peel as garnish along with a shiso leaf.

WATERMELON-SHISO SYRUP: Combine 2 cups sugar, 1 cup chopped watermelon, and 3 to 4 shiso leaves in a blender and blend on high for 1 minute. Strain and refrigerate the syrup for up to 2 weeks.

APERITIVO FIZZ

FOLK

823 MERIDIAN STREET

This has been a house favorite ever since inception," says beverage director Jordan Spaulding. "Lots of bright floral notes dance around under a big tangy first sip. Focused on replicating both depth of flavor and mouthfeel of a classic shaken Amaro Fizz."

GLASSWARE: Collins glass

GARNISH: Grapefruit peel

- 1 oz. Dhōs Bittersweet
- 1 oz. Grapefruit Cordial (see recipe)
- 1 oz. fresh lemon juice
- ½ oz. simple syrup
- ⅜ oz. Folk Ginger Syrup (see recipe)
- ½ oz. Jack Rudy Cocktail Co. Classic Tonic Syrup
- Seltzer, to top

1. Combine all of the ingredients, except for the seltzer, in a shaker tin with ice and shake until the tin is ice cold.

2. Strain the cocktail over fresh ice into a collins glass.

3. Top with a splash of seltzer.

4. Express a grapefruit peel over the mocktail, then add the peel as garnish.

FOLK GINGER SYRUP: In a saucepan, combine 1½ parts sugar to 1 part raw ginger juice and bring to a simmer, stirring until the sugar is dissolved. Allow the syrup to cool.

GRAPEFRUIT CORDIAL:
In a pan, toast 25 grams pink peppercorns, 50 grams juniper berries, and 8 cloves. Add in 976 ml (33 oz.) water and 750 grams grapefruit peels and bring the mixture to a simmer. Turn off the heat and add in 15 dried lavender flowers, then vacuum-seal all of the ingredients in a bag and store it in the refrigerator for 24 hours. Strain the liquid back into a pan and heat it again. Add in 450 grams sugar and 1,183 ml (40 oz.) vegetable glycerin and stir to combine. Keep refrigerated.

MORIR SOÑANDO

TANTÍSIMO

Morir soñando means "to die dreaming" in Spanish. "We love this drink from the Dominican Republic," says Ana Aguilar. "Our version uses house-made evaporated milk—we think it gives us the creamiest and freshest version possible. It's a crowd pleaser!"

GLASSWARE: **Collins glass**

GARNISH: **Orange zest**

- **5 oz. fresh orange juice**
- **1 oz. Evaporated Milk (see recipe)**
- **¾ oz. raw sugar simple syrup**
- **Barspoon clear vanilla**

1. Add all of the ingredients to a cocktail shaker with ice.

2. Shake for 10 to 15 seconds until chilled and creamy.

3. Pour the cocktail into a collins glass with the ice from the shaker. This helps create a crushed ice effect. Add more ice if needed.

4. Garnish with freshly grated orange zest.

EVAPORATED MILK: Add high-quality whole milk, as needed, to a saucepan. Simmering, reduce the milk's volume by half. Remove it from heat and allow it to cool.

WITBIER SHANDY

AUDREY/JUNE
809 MERIDIAN STREET

E ric Jeffus (see his interview on page 310) puts as much time and effort into zero-proof pairings and drink options as he does the boozy ones at Sean Brock's East Nashville restaurants, and it absolutely shows. Though many might be far too complicated to replicate at home, here's a fun beer lovers' NA option, with a delightful homemade shandy base.

GLASSWARE: Beer glass

GARNISH: Freshly ground coriander seeds

- 6 oz. Athletic Brewing Run Wild IPA (NA)
- 4 oz. Shandy Base (see recipe)

1. Combine the ingredients in a beer glass and add ice to fill.

2. Garnish with coriander seeds, coarsely ground in a spice grinder or using a mortar and pestle.

SHANDY BASE: Combine equal parts by volume of Acidified Orange Juice (see recipe), Coriander Syrup (see recipe), and Maypop Sparkling Water.

ACIDIFIED ORANGE JUICE: For every 100 ml of freshly squeezed orange juice, add 6 grams citric acid powder, and stir vigorously to combine.

CORIANDER SYRUP: Combine 3 cups white sugar, 3 cups water, and 3 tablespoons coriander seeds in a saucepan and bring the mixture to a boil. Turn down the heat and simmer 15 to 20 minutes, then blend the mixture in a blender (crank it for at least a couple minutes). Fine-strain the syrup to remove fine particles.

MOONSHINE AND
BUSHWACKERS

THE CLASSIC NASHVILLE BUSHWACKER

THE FLORIDA WAY

BLACKBERRY MOUNTAIN TEA

OLE SMOKY PEPPERMINT WHITE RUSSIAN

NASHVILLE MOONSHINE PUNCH

JAVA NICE DAY

SOUTHERN PEACH PIE

EAST NASHVILLE SUNRISE

RYMAN REFRESHER

Moonshine, a high-proof distilled spirit once produced illicitly, almost synonymous with East Tennessee, has a storied history in the South. It is said that in the mid-1700s, Irish and Scottish immigrants settled in the Smoky Mountains, bringing with them their Celtic music, which later morphed into bluegrass, and their traditions of distilling whiskey.

"Moonshining" was established when the United States ordered a tax on the sale of alcohol and drove distilling underground. In order to duck paying the hefty taxes, the first moonshiners were extremely methodical in their practices, both in production and distribution. Of course, the term "moonshining" and "moonshine" both got their names from the work of distilling and selling at night, under the light of the moon. Soon after, flocks of farmers throughout the Smokies took up moonshining to make extra cash from their surplus corn crops.

When federal Prohibition was enacted in 1920, the illegal distillation and sales of alcohol spread nationwide. It was rumored that Al Capone himself stashed his illicit spirits somewhere in the Smoky Mountains before transporting them to Chicago.

A change in state law in Tennessee in 2009 paved the way for several moonshine distilleries to open up in Tennessee's other major tourist hub, Gatlinburg. That city allows distilleries to charge a $5 tasting fee, which can be applied to purchases in a distillery gift shop.

Today, of course, new legal moonshine products have found their way into Nashville's mainstream bars. It's not uncommon to find this potent drink served straight or flavor-infused in a variety of directions.

Ole Smoky has made their legal 'shine approachable to the masses, offering a rainbow of fun flavors in their popular tasting rooms in

Tennessee's tourist meccas Gatlinburg, Pigeon Forge, and Downtown Nashville. The Music City Ole Smoky outpost is a party, sharing a 30,000-square-foot complex at 6th and Peabody with YeeHaw Brewing. The company's co-founder, Joe Baker, used a century-old family recipe that he fine-tuned to launch the brand back in 2010, shortly after the state made moonshine legal. As the first legal moonshine in East Tennessee, the brand has grown exponentially in the past decade.

Another star of Nashville's non-whiskey scene is the Bushwacker. Essentially, a chocolatey, boozy milkshake, the Bushwacker is a delightfully indulgent concoction that combines cream of coconut, coffee liqueur, and dark rum, all topped off with a generous squirt of whipped cream. It's a dessert, a drink, and an experience all in one. And if you insist on whiskey, there are several recipes around town that include that, too. But if you're looking to sip on something iconic to Music City that isn't whiskey, say hello to Moonshine and the delightful Bushwacker.

WHERE TO GET GREAT BUSHWACKERS IN NASHVILLE

BROADWAY BREWPUB & GRUB
1900 BROADWAY

M.L. ROSE CRAFT BEER & BURGERS
(MULTIPLE LOCATIONS)

EDLEY'S BAR-B-QUE
(MULTIPLE LOCATIONS)

THE RED DOOR SALOON
(MIDTOWN AND EAST NASHVILLE)

REBAR AT THE DAM
3248 BLACKWOOD DRIVE

THE CLASSIC NASHVILLE BUSHWHACKER

M.L. ROSE CRAFT BEER & BURGERS

I s it a milkshake or is it a cocktail? Nashville is not the birthplace of many iconic cocktails (including this one), but Music City still has stories staking a claim on the adult honky-tonk milkshake. The creamy, chocolatey concoction is irresistibly delicious, and a staple for first-time Nashville visitors.

✳

GLASSWARE: Hurricane glass

- 1 oz. dark rum
- 1 oz. Kahlúa
- 1 oz. crème de cacao
- 2 oz. cream of coconut
- 2 oz. half-and-half
- 1 cup ice

1. Chill a hurricane glass. Combine all of the ingredients in a blender and blend until smooth.

2. Pour the drink into the chilled hurricane glass.

THE FLORIDA WAY

Pensacola natives say this is the only Bushwacker recipe you should follow.

GLASSWARE: Hurricane glass

GARNISH: Whipped cream, maraschino cherry, grated nutmeg

- 12 oz. vodka
- ½ oz. rum
- ½ oz. Baileys Original Irish Cream
- ½ oz. Kahlúa
- ½ oz. amaretto liqueur
- ½ oz. chocolate liqueur
- ½ oz. Frangelico
- ½ oz. Coco López Cream of Coconut

1. Combine all of the ingredients in a blender with ice and blend until the mixture has the consistency of a milkshake, adding ice as needed.

2. Pour the cocktail into hurricane glasses and garnish with whipped cream, cherries, and freshly grated nutmeg.

BLACKBERRY MOUNTAIN TEA

THE SOUTHERN STEAK & OYSTER
150 3RD AVENUE SOUTH

Think Nashville staple and post-church picnic fruit tea, but make it boozy. A surefire porch-sippin' favorite from TomKats Hospitality's downtown seafood and steak haven, The Southern Steak & Oyster.

✳

GLASSWARE: Collins glass
GARNISH: Fresh blackberries, lemon wedge

- **2½ oz. Ole Smoky Blackberry Moonshine**
- **2½ oz. sweet tea**
- **Lemonade, to top**

1. Add ice to a collins glass.

2. Add the moonshine and tea, top with lemonade, and stir.

3. Garnish with fresh blackberries and a lemon wedge.

OLE SMOKY PEPPERMINT WHITE RUSSIAN

OLE SMOKY AT 6TH AND PEABODY
423 6TH AVENUE SOUTH

When the Nashville heat fades and winter days keep us bundled up in layers and blankets, the afterburn of moonshine will bring a little heat. As if a classic White Russian wasn't already decadent enough, try switching out the standard spirit for Ole Smoky Peppermint Moonshine and a crushed candy cane rim to get into the festive holiday spirit. Pairs well with a fire cracking in the fireplace and a great wintertime playlist.

GLASSWARE: **Rocks glass**

- **Candy cane, crushed, for the rim**
- **2 oz. Ole Smoky Peppermint Moonshine**
- **¾ oz. coffee liqueur**
- **¾ oz. half-and-half**

1. Wet the rim of a rocks glass with water then dip the glass in crushed candy cane bits.

2. Combine all of the ingredients in a mixing glass and mix well.

3. Serve on the rocks.

NASHVILLE MOONSHINE PUNCH

This sweet drink uses Ole Smoky Hunch Punch Lightnin', a potent concoction blending their smooth moonshine with a summery blend of juice from oranges, pineapples, and cherries.

GLASSWARE: **Mason jar**

GARNISH: **Cherry, lemon wedge**

- **2 oz. Ole Smoky Hunch Punch Lightnin'**
- **2 oz. fresh pineapple juice**
- **2 oz. tart cherry juice**
- **1 oz. cranberry juice**
- **1 oz. apple juice**

1. Fill a shaker halfway with ice then add all of the ingredients to the shaker.

2. Shake for about 15 seconds.

3. Fill a mason jar with ice and, using a Hawthorne strainer, strain the cocktail into the mason jar.

4. Garnish with a cherry and lemon.

JAVA NICE DAY

ACME FEED & SEED
101 BROADWAY

This frozen moonshine cocktail from Lisa Karkos at Acme Feed & Seed is giving major beachside Espresso Martini vibes with a Tennessee twang. This is a great brunch-time indulgence or summer poolside treat for a crowd. This recipe yields multiple servings.

GLASSWARE: 12 oz. cup

- **4½ oz. Ole Smoky Mountain Java Coffee Cream Liqueur**
- **4½ oz. Slow & Low Coffee Old-Fashioned**
- **4½ oz. cold water**
- **4½ oz. Switters Iced Coffee Middle Ground**
- **1¼ oz. coffee cordial**
- **1 oz. simple syrup**

1. In a blender, add ice then all of the ingredients.

2. Blend to your desired consistency.

3. Pour the cocktail into 12 oz. cups.

SOUTHERN PEACH PIE

EAST TASTY CANDY COMPANY

There's nothing quite like going to the farmers market and picking up fresh peaches for your pie," says Jordan Tepper, of the East Tasty Candy Company. "Here that sentiment translates into a simple and sweet cocktail, just like life should be." For the spirits, use peach moonshine, peach pie moonshine, or peach cobbler moonshine.

GLASSWARE: Mason jar

GARNISH: Mint sprig

- 4 oz. ginger ale
- 2 oz. peach moonshine
- 1 oz. Mint Simple Syrup (see recipe)

1. Add all of the ingredients in a mason jar.

2. Garnish with a sprig of fresh mint.

MINT SIMPLE SYRUP: In a small saucepan over medium heat, combine 1 cup water, 1 cup sugar, and 1½ cups mint leaves and bring the mixture to a simmer, stirring until all of the sugar is dissolved. Remove the syrup from heat and allow it to cool. Strain the syrup before using.

EAST NASHVILLE SUNRISE

EAST TASTY CANDY COMPANY

T here's nothing like leaving a bar after a long night," says Jordan Tepper, "and the sun is rising, but you still have to go to work. This is a sweet, fruity drink."

GLASSWARE: Mason jar

GARNISH: Cherry, lemon wheel

- 2 oz. fresh orange juice
- 2 oz. fresh pineapple juice
- 1 oz. Ole Smoky Sour Watermelon Moonshine
- 1 oz. TC Craft Blanco Tequila
- ½ oz. grenadine

1. Combine all of the ingredients in a mason jar with ice.

2. Garnish with a cherry and lemon wheel.

RYMAN REFRESHER

EAST TASTY CANDY COMPANY

This drink is for "when you need a strong, refreshing cocktail, but you don't want others to know you are drinking a cocktail," says Jordan Tepper. "This is named after the historic Ryman, which of course used to be a church."

---- ✳ ----

GLASSWARE: Footed rocks glass

GARNISH: Lime wedge

- 1 oz. lemon/citron vodka
- 1 oz. Corsair American Gin

- 6 oz. ginger beer
- Squeeze of fresh lime juice

1. Add all of the ingredients, except for the lime juice, to a rocks glass.
2. Add a squeeze of lime juice. Garnish with a lime wedge.

BRUNCH, BACHELORETTES, AND ROOFTOPS: THE NEW NASHVILLE

SOUTHERN BOURBON
MILK PUNCH

PERSIMMON GIN FIZZ

BRÛLÉED BANANA
DAIQUIRI

L ove it or hate it, partying is sort of the religion of New Nashville. The spirit of this wild new phase that's developed over the last decade is perhaps best embodied in the city's vibrant trifecta of brunch, bachelorette parties, and rooftop hangouts.

Sunday brunch has been elevated to an art form here with a myriad of eateries offering their bespoke takes on Southern classics, and more hot chicken and waffles than you can shake a stick at.

On any day of the week, it's a common occurrence to see merry bands of bachelorettes parading down Broadway, sipping cocktails and soaking in the city's infectious energy.

From Mimosas, over-the-top Bloody Marys, and Espresso Martinis at brunch, to after-dark drinks on a buzzing rooftop bar, in New Nashville, it's clear that brunch, bachelorettes, party buses, and rooftop soirees are a central part of the city's culture as a tourist destination. Woo!

GREAT HOTEL ROOFTOP BARS TO VISIT IN NASHVILLE

LA JACKSON (THOMPSON NASHVILLE HOTEL)
401 11TH AVENUE SOUTH

RARE BIRD (NOELLE HOTEL NASHVILLE)
200 4TH AVENUE NORTH

DENIM (THE JOSEPH, A LUXURY COLLECTION HOTEL)
401 KOREAN VETERANS BOULEVARD

BOBBY HOTEL ROOFTOP LOUNGE
230 4TH AVENUE NORTH

WHITE LIMOZEEN (GRADUATE NASHVILLE)
101 20TH AVENUE NORTH

HARRIET'S ROOFTOP (1 HOTEL NASHVILLE)
710 DEMONBREUN STREET

LOU/NA (GRAND HYATT NASHVILLE)
1000 BROADWAY

THE POOL CLUB AT VIRGIN HOTELS NASHVILLE
1 MUSIC SQUARE

HEIRLOOM (HOLSTON HOUSE NASHVILLE)
118 7TH AVENUE NORTH

Rare Bird

SOUTHERN BOURBON MILK PUNCH

New Orleans claims the bragging rights for its traditional Brandy Milk Punch, a Sunday brunch staple. But Nashville-based food photographer and blogger Phillip Fryman (@southernfatty) takes the recipe back to his Kentucky roots, building off bourbon, but he changes out the bourbon when he wants alternatives: "I add a bit of Fernet-Branca to give a bit of herbal mint background to the drink at night, or I use brandy for something you might not usually lean toward when mixing up cocktails."

GLASSWARE: Rocks glass

- 2 oz. whole milk, whole
- 1½ oz. Kentucky bourbon
- ½ oz. honey
- ½ teaspoon pure vanilla extract
- ⅛ teaspoon nutmeg, freshly grated

- Nutmeg, freshly grated, for the rim
- Cinnamon, freshly grated, for the rim
- Cardamom, freshly grated, for the rim

1. In a cocktail shaker with ice, combine all of the ingredients except for the spices for the rim.

2. Shake very well for at least 30 seconds.

3. Wet the rim of a rocks glass then dip the glass in the mixture of grated spices.

4. Pour the cocktail into the glass filled with crushed ice.

PERSIMMON GIN FIZZ

A nother take on a classic from Phillip Fryman, this time with a spin featuring the winter fruit persimmon and a bubbly ginger bite. Of course, the Gin Fizz is a favorite New Orleans brunch companion, with a rich history dating back to the mid-nineteenth century. This version will level up your at-home brunch game for sure.

GLASSWARE: Coupe glass

GARNISH: Sliced persimmon, star anise

- **3 oz. Hendrick's Gin**
- **¾ oz. Persimmon Simple Syrup (see recipe)**
- **1 egg white**
- **½ teaspoon fresh lemon juice**
- **Bundaberg Ginger Beer, to top**
- **Orange bitters, as needed**

1. Combine the gin, simple syrup, egg white, and lemon juice in a cocktail shaker and shake hard for 30 seconds.

2. Fill the shaker halfway with ice and shake for vigorously for 1 minute.

3. Strain the cocktail into a coupe and garnish with sliced persimmon and star anise.

4. Top with a splash of ginger beer and a few shakes of orange bitters.

PERSIMMON SIMPLE SYRUP: In a saucepan, combine 1 cup sugar, 1 cup water, and 1 sliced persimmon and bring the mixture to a boil. Boil for 4 to 5 minutes. Remove from heat and let the syrup cool completely. Strain.

BRÛLÉED BANANA DAIQUIRI

"I scream, you scream, we all scream for . . . Daiquiris! Pretty sure that's how it goes," says Phillip Fryman. "Frozen bananas at amusement parks, smoothies to get your sunny day started, banana bread to use up those not so pretty picks—this fruit screams summer to me, so why not turn it into a nice frozen draaaaank?! Moving in the direction of the frozen park bananas that I grew up having at parks, we're torching some honey and dark rum on top of this sundae to turn things up a bit." You can substitute cream for the half-and-half for a richer cocktail.

GLASSWARE: **Coupe or margarita glass**

GARNISH: **Slice of Brûléed Banana (see recipe)**

- **Brûléed Banana (see recipe)**
- **2 oz. white rum**
- **2 to 4 tablespoons simple syrup**
- **1 tablespoon fresh lime juice**
- **¼ teaspoon vanilla extract**
- **1 oz. half-and-half**

1. Combine the Brûléed Banana halves with the remaining ingredients, except for the half-and-half, in a blender with 3 cups ice and blend until smooth.

2. Add the half-and-half and pulse to just combine.

3. Pour the cocktail into a coupe or margarita glass and garnish with a slice of Brûléed Banana.

BRÛLÉED BANANA: Heat a grill or skillet over medium/medium-high heat. Slice a banana with the peel still on in half lengthwise, leaving you with two long halves. In a small bowl, combine 1 oz. dark rum and 1 tablespoon honey. Use a brush to cover the cut sides of the banana halves (not the peel) generously with the honey-rum mixture. Grill the exposed banana until caramelized grill marks show, about 3 to 4 minutes. Remove the banana halves from heat and plate with the banana flesh face up. Brush additional honey-rum mixture on the banana halves. Use a constantly moving kitchen torch to brûlée the tops gently, taking care to not burn the topping. Allow bananas to cool completely and remove the peels before use.

MELTING POT: NASHVILLE'S OTHER NEIGHBORHOODS

VIOLET, YOU'RE TURNING VIOLET	CHERRY WHISKEY SOUR
THE RYMAN	BRANDY ALEJANDRO
FRANKLIN FIZZ	PISCO SOUR
EDEN	THE CORNER'S DILEMMA
SELENA	STILL NOT A PLAYER
THE ONLY TENN I SEE	THUNDERBIRD
SPICY STRAWBERRY RYE	MAGIC STICK
JAM SESSION	THE GOLD RUSH
SMOOTH SAILING	
OSTARA	

E ven though the pandemic slowed the growth of Nashville a bit, the latest reports say that 100 new residents are still moving to Nashville every day, whether to one of the dozens of new apartments popping up downtown, or into the suburbs or exurbs. From Hendersonville, Salemtown, and North Nashville, to Germantown, Brentwood, and Franklin, Nashville's neighborhoods showcase a unique blend of cultures. Venture down Nolensville Road and immerse yourself in the vibrant Latin American community, where the air is saturated with the tempting aroma of authentic pupusas and arepas. You can find a slice of "Little Kurdistan" tucked away in the city, serving mouthwatering dolmas and baklava, testament to the burgeoning Middle Eastern population in Middle Tennessee. The historic Jefferson Street stands testament to Nashville's African American history and its profound influence on the city's music scene.

VIOLET, YOU'RE TURNING VIOLET

MASON BAR
2100 WEST END AVENUE

Our vision was to make a light, refreshing drink that utilizes fresh, seasonal ingredients," says Jereme Pozin, director of food and beverage at Loews Vanderbilt Hotel, which is the building housing Mason Bar. "The juniper-forward gin, house-made lavender syrup, and hand-squeezed lemon juice combine for a springtime essence, while the crème de violette makes for a smooth finish. The lavender-smoke-filled bubble adds an exciting sensorial element, as when it pops, you're compelled to breathe in the swirling, floral aroma that complements the garden-inspired flavors of the cocktail."

GLASSWARE: Coupe or martini glass

GARNISH: Sprig of lavender, sweet violet purple flower

- 1½ oz. Hendrick's Gin
- 1½ oz. fresh lemon juice
- 1 oz. Lavender Simple Syrup (see recipe)
- ½ oz. crème de violette

1. Chill a coupe or martini glass. Combine all of the ingredients in a cocktail shaker with ice and shake well.

2. Strain the cocktail into the chilled coupe or martini glass.

3. Garnish with fresh lavender and a purple flower.

4. If you have the equipment, use a Flavour Blaster or Flavour Blaster Mini to top the glass with a lavender smoke bubble.

LAVENDER SIMPLE SYRUP: In a small saucepan over medium heat, combine 1 cup water, 1 cup sugar, and 3 tablespoons lavender buds and bring the mixture to a simmer. Stir until the sugar is dissolved and remove the syrup from heat. Allow the syrup to cool completely and strain.

THE RYMAN

1799 KITCHEN & COCKTAILS
130 2ND AVENUE NORTH, FRANKLIN

L ocated within the charming Harpeth Hotel in downtown Franklin, 1799 Kitchen & Cocktails serves up fresh takes on Southern staples, prime steaks and chops, and a truly extensive list of wine and spirits. This cocktail is a nod to a Nashville destination that doesn't need an introduction.

GLASSWARE: Rocks glass
GARNISH: Lemon wheel, maraschino cherry

- 2 oz. Sazerac Rye
- ½ oz. dry curaçao
- ½ oz. fresh lemon juice
- ½ oz. orgeat
- ½ oz. demerara syrup
- 6 to 8 dashes Angostura bitters, to top

1. Add all of the ingredients, except for the bitters, to a shaker.

2. Shake with ice, then strain over ice into a rocks glass.

3. Top with the Angostura bitters.

4. Garnish with a lemon wheel and a maraschino cherry on a skewer.

FRANKLIN FIZZ

1799 KITCHEN & COCKTAILS
130 2ND AVENUE NORTH, FRANKLIN

The Franklin Fizz was an addition to the Harpeth Hotel's fall drink lineup, and it's an easy sipper, equally enjoyed in the bar, in the courtyard, or in the lobby with live music accompaniment.

GLASSWARE: Coupe glass

GARNISH: Edible flower

- 1 oz. Aperol
- 1 oz. dry gin
- ¾ oz. fresh lemon juice
- ½ oz. orgeat
- 1 egg white

1. Add all of the ingredients to a shaker and dry-shake.

2. Add ice and shake again until the shaker is cold.

3. Double-strain the cocktail into a coupe and garnish with an edible flower.

EDEN

Hathorne's beverage director, Hayley Teague, loves championing great women-owned spirits companies. Melissa Katrincic is the creator and owner of Durham Distillery, the first and only American woman distiller inducted into the Gin Guild of the UK. The Kinship showcases a stunning purple to pink hue that is perfect for Hayley's own super fun aesthetic and signature flower garnishes.

GLASSWARE: Wineglass

GARNISH: Bitter Violet Foam (see recipe), edible flowers

- 1½ oz. Conniption Kinship Gin
- ¾ oz. Padró & Co. Blanco Reserva Vermouth
- ½ oz. crème de violette
- ¼ oz. simple syrup
- ¼ oz. fresh lemon juice
- 2 dashes orange bitters
- 2 to 3 oz. cava, to top

1. Combine all of the ingredients, except for the cava, in a wineglass.

2. Top with the cava.

3. Garnish with the foam and edible flowers.

BITTER VIOLET FOAM: Whisk 3 egg whites, 2¼ oz. lemon juice, 2¼ oz. grapefruit juice, 2¼ oz. simple syrup, 1 oz. crème de violette, and 2 drops orange oil together and pour the mixture into an iSi canister. Give it two charges. Test before topping the cocktail.

SELENA

HATHORNE
4708 CHARLOTTE AVENUE

The Selena may read like a spicy Margarita," says Hayley Teague, "but it doesn't exactly taste like one. With a rim of ancho chile powder and sea salt, plus ancho pepper–infused dry curaçao, this tart, easy-to-drink refresher is much more like the Margarita's sophisticated aunt." For the smoked pineapple juice, Hayley uses a jar and a smoking gun.

GLASSWARE: Collins glass

GARNISH: Large edible flower

- Ancho chile powder, for the rim
- Sea salt, for the rim
- 1½ oz. reposado tequila
- 1½ oz. Smoked Pineapple Juice (see recipe)
- ½ oz. Ancho-Infused Dry Curaçao (see recipe)
- ½ oz. Monin Passion Fruit Syrup
- ½ oz. fresh lime juice

1. Wet the rim of a collins glass with water then dip the glass in ancho chile powder and sea salt.

2. Add the remaining ingredients to a shaker tin with ice and shake.

3. Pour the cocktail into the collins glass.

4. Garnish with a large edible flower.

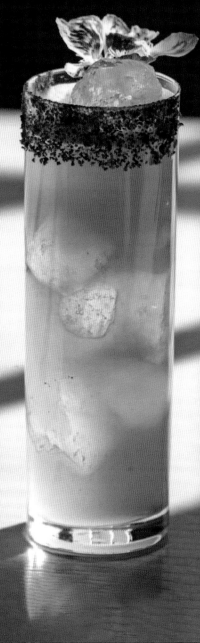

Ancho-Infused Dry Curaçao:

Put ancho chile peppers, to taste, in a nonreactive container. Pour dry curaçao over the chiles. Cover the container and let the mixture sit for 48 hours. Strain and transfer to a bottle.

Smoked Pineapple Juice:

Fill a large jar about two-thirds of the way with fresh pineapple juice. Using a smoking gun filled with applewood chips, fill the container with thick smoke. Cover the jar and let it sit until the juice absorbs all of the smoke.

THE ONLY TENN I SEE

GRANDPA BAR
1501 HERMAN STREET SUITE 123

This social sipper can be found at Grandpa Bar in the Marathon Village neighborhood of Nashville, which doubles as a cozy coffee shop during the day and whiskey-centric cocktail bar at night. The Only Tenn I See is a sweeter Old Fashioned inspired by the welcoming nature of Nashville. The finished color is Tennessee Volunteers orange. "What's more soul-warming than coffee and whiskey?" says Mike Rosenthal, owner of Grandpa Bar.

GLASSWARE: Rocks glass

GARNISH: Amarena cherry, orange slice,
mini Tennessee flag toothpick

- 2 oz. Nelson's Green Brier Tennessee Whiskey
- 4 dashes Angostura bitters
- ⅓ oz. Goo Goo Syrup (see recipe)
- Spritz of orange oil

1. Combine all of the ingredients, except for the orange oil, in a mixing glass with ice and stir for 30 seconds.

2. Strain the cocktail over a big, clear ice cube into a rocks glass.

3. Spritz with orange oil (or express a fresh orange peel).

4. Garnish with a toothpick flag, Amarena cherry, and orange slice.

GOO GOO SYRUP: In 10-second increments, microwave 25 grams creamy peanut butter until melted. In a small saucepan over medium heat, combine 175 grams water and 250 grams organic cane sugar and stir until the sugar is dissolved. Lower the heat to low, add 30 grams marshmallows and stir until the marshmallows are dissolved. Add the melted peanut butter, 25 grams caramel sauce, 15 grams chocolate sauce, and a pinch Himalayan salt, stirring until combined. Strain the syrup through cheesecloth or a coffee filter and bottle. Store it in the refrigerator for 2 weeks.

SPICY STRAWBERRY RYE

MÈRE BULLES
5201 MARYLAND WAY, BRENTWOOD

In 1937, J. Truman Ward, then the owner of Nashville's WLAC radio, bought 100 acres of stump land on a one-lane gravel road in Brentwood about 300 yards south of Old Hickory Boulevard. Ward loved horses all his life and wanted to have a place to keep a couple of pleasure horses for himself, his wife, Mary, and son, Jimmy. He named the farm Maryland in honor of his wife. By 1945 he had purchased additional land so that Maryland Farm grew to 400 acres. The farm was home to American Ace, the leading sire of the American Saddlebred horse breed, making it nationally known. The Wards enjoyed entertaining, and Maryland Manor was the scene of many festive occasions and several weddings. This tradition is continued today, according to Kevin Crowley, with so many special occasions at Mère Bulles, which also features a bar honoring local traditions. This cocktail goes down easy, with strawberry serrano shrub, with the summer fruit sweetness of Nolensville-based Wheeler's Raid #4.

GLASSWARE: Rocks glass

GARNISH: Dehydrated lime wheel

- 1¾ oz. Wheeler's Raid Original Blend Rye 04
- 1 oz. Carpano Antica Formula Vermouth
- ¾ oz. Strawberry Serrano Shrub (see recipe)
- Squeeze of fresh lime juice

1. Combine all of the ingredients in a cocktail shaker.

2. Add ice and shake until chilled.

3. Dirty-dump (pour all of the liquid and ice) into a rocks glass and top with fresh ice.

4. Garnish with a dehydrated lime wheel.

STRAWBERRY SERRANO SHRUB: Add 8 cups white vinegar and 8 cups white sugar to a large Cambro container with a lid. Carefully peel 8 limes, trying not to remove too much pith. Add the peels to the mixture. Halve the limes and juice them into the mixture. Roughly chop 10 to 12 serrano peppers and add them to the mixture. Wash 4 clamshell containers of strawberries, then trim the strawberries and cut them into quarters. Mix everything together and let it sit for a minimum of 3 days, stirring daily. The shrub is shelf stable.

JAM SESSION

MÈRE BULLES
5201 MARYLAND WAY, BRENTWOOD

Aptly named for a Music City cocktail, the Jam Session blends pine-forward botanical gin with a house grenadine and the real star: strawberry basil cabernet jam. The result is like a hug from a sweet Southern grandma at a post-church Sunday supper, says Mags Humbracht of Mère Bulles.

GLASSWARE: Coupe glass

GARNISH: Dehydrated lime wheel

- 2 oz. Gray Whale Gin
- ¾ oz. Strawberry Basil Cabernet Jam (see recipe)
- ½ oz. fresh lime juice
- ¼ oz. House Grenadine (see recipe)

1. Add all of the ingredients to a shaker.

2. Add ice and shake until chilled.

3. Strain the cocktail into a coupe glass and garnish with a dehydrated lime wheel.

HOUSE GRENADINE: Combine 32 oz. POM 100% Pomegranate Juice and 2 cups sugar in a saucepan. Bring the mixture to a boil and immediately remove from heat. Stir until the sugar is dissolved. Allow the grenadine to cool before using.

STRAWBERRY BASIL CABERNET JAM: Hull (gently remove the stems from) 1 clamshell of strawberries. Halve the strawberries, and soak them and 1 clamshell of raspberries in 3 cups sugar for at least 20 minutes. Add the fruit-and-sugar mixture to a pot with 1 oz. lemon juice and 1 bottle Drumheller Cabernet Sauvignon and stir thoroughly. Bring the mixture to a boil over medium heat, stirring constantly. When a white foam appears, turn off the heat and let the mixture cool. Skim the white foam from the top. Add 3 stalks of basil. Return the mixture to heat and bring it back to a boil. Once it boils, turn off the heat again. Press the syrup through a sieve to remove solids.

SMOOTH SAILING

COMMON GROUND
4001 CHARLOTTE AVENUE

After enjoying one of these cocktails," says Wes Taylor, of Common Ground, "the rest of your day will surely be 'Smooth Sailing.'"

GLASSWARE: Rocks glass

GARNISH: Mint bouquet

- 2 oz. Gordon's London Dry Gin
- ¾ oz. Coconut Grapefruit Cordial (see recipe)
- ½ oz. fresh lime juice
- ¼ oz. simple syrup
- ½ oz. John D. Taylor's Velvet Falernum

1. Combine all of the ingredients in a shaker tin, add ice, and shake vigorously for 5 seconds.

2. Strain the cocktail into a rocks glass over fresh ice cubes.

3. Garnish with a large bouquet of mint.

COCONUT GRAPEFRUIT CORDIAL: In a medium saucepan over medium heat, add 1 (16 oz.) bottle or can of coconut water, 1 cup sugar, and 2 grapefruit peels and bring the mixture to a boil. Kill the heat and whisk to fully dissolve the sugar. Pass the mixture through a fine-mesh strainer to remove the grapefruit peels. Add fresh grapefruit juice (half the weight of the liquid) and stir to combine. Label, date, and store the cordial in the refrigerator for up to 2 weeks.

BAR SPOTLIGHT: ATTABOY

8 MCFERRIN AVENUE

Nashville got its own outpost of the top-shelf NYC cocktail bar by the same name back in 2017, and this Attaboy was a game-changer. This one's a little easier to find than its New York counterpart, with signage on the side of the nondescript building. Just knock on the door, wait for it to open, and a host will greet you and ask how many are in your party. Then, you're either seated or given a wait time. Once inside, there's no menu to peruse. The highly trained staff just ask a few questions to hone in on exactly what each guest is in the mood for on any given night, and then they handle it from there.

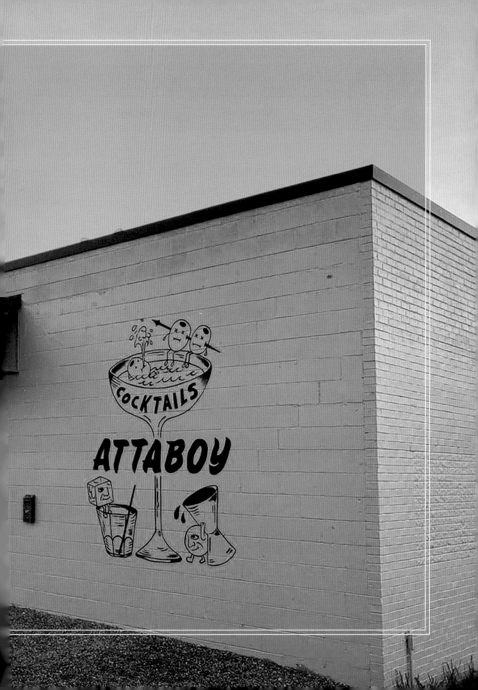

OSTARA

ATTABOY
8 MCFERRIN AVENUE

The idea here is to combine an early spring ingredient—dandelion—with a late spring ingredient—rhubarb—and an early summer ingredient—strawberry—as a celebration of the transition from spring to summer in a reliable Collins cocktail format," says Erik Anthony Garcia, bartender at Attaboy. "Rhubarb pie and dandelion wine should be as familiar to any born-and-bred Southerner."

GLASSWARE: Collins glass

GARNISH: Strawberry half

- 1 to 2 strawberries, hulled
- ¾ oz. fresh lemon juice
- ¾ oz. simple syrup
- ½ oz. Suze L'Originale

- 1 oz. Fords London Dry Gin
- ½ oz. Giffard Rhubarbe Liqueur
- Soda water, to top

1. In a mixing glass, muddle 1 or 2 strawberries.

2. Add the remaining ingredients, except for the soda water, and shake very briefly with ice.

3. Strain the cocktail over ice into a collins glass while simultaneously adding soda water.

4. Garnish with half a strawberry.

CHERRY WHISKEY SOUR

Phillip Fryman (@southernfatty online) shares a riff on the Whiskey Sour with a summer cherry kick. Choose from Tennessee whiskey or Kentucky bourbon to make it your own.

GLASSWARE: Coupe glass

GARNISH: Skewered cherries

- 2¼ oz. bourbon
- ¾ oz. fresh lemon juice
- ½ oz. simple syrup
- 1 teaspoon cherry juice
- 1 egg white

1. Combine the bourbon, lemon juice, simple syrup, and cherry juice in a cocktail shaker with 5 to 6 ice cubes and shake well for 30 seconds.

2. Strain out the ice and return the cocktail to the shaker without ice.

3. Add the egg white and shake as vigorously as possible for an entire minute to build foam.

4. Pour the cocktail into a coupe and garnish with skewered cherries.

BRANDY ALEJANDRO

This is Tantísimo's take on a Brandy Alexander, but with a bit of aged tequila. Recipe by Ana Aguilar, Don McGreevy, and Heather Sherman.

GLASSWARE: Coupe glass

GARNISH: Freshly grated nutmeg

- 1 oz. cream
- 1 oz. crème de cacao
- ¾ oz. Tequila Corrido Reposado
- ¾ oz. Copper & Kings American Craft Brandy
- Barspoon Pajarote Ponche de Chocolate (optional)

1. Chill a coupe glass. Add all of the ingredients to a cocktail shaker with ice.

2. Shake well.

3. Strain the cocktail into the chilled coupe.

4. Garnish with freshly grated nutmeg.

PISCO SOUR

Crowd-favorite Mexicana-owned "Spainglish Shop" Tantísimo is a pandemic-born passion project by the talented Ana Aguilar, which originally began by providing pastries for other pop-ups. She eventually added savory items to her menu, providing street-style Mexican snacks, family meals, and, still, her excellent farm-to-table pastry items. All in all, Ana is a storyteller through her food, acting, and her drinks. Here's her straightforward take on the classic Pisco Sour.

GLASSWARE: Coupe glass

GARNISH: 3 to 5 drops Angostura bitters

- 1¾ oz. Pisco 100 Acholado
- 1 oz. raw sugar simple syrup
- ½ oz. fresh lime juice
- ½ oz. fresh lemon juice
- ½ oz. egg white

1. Chill a coupe glass. Add all of the ingredients to a cocktail shaker and give it a dry shake for at least 10 to 15 seconds to emulsify the egg white.

2. Add ice and shake thoroughly.

3. Strain the cocktail into the chilled coupe, making sure to include the layer of foam over the top.

4. Carefully garnish with Angostura bitters.

ADAM SLOAN,
SOUNDTRACK MY DRINK

Adam Sloan is the owner of @SoundtrackMyDrink, which began as a fun hobby Instagram account and quickly grew into a full-time platform where Adam pairs his original cocktail recipes with specific songs. Adam also serves as a consultant and recipe developer, playlist curator, and home bar concierge. His recipes have an experimental quality to them that feels adventurous, and he's adept at crafting creative captions that connect the tunes to the booze in unexpected ways. Here he is in his own words.

How did @SoundtrackMyDrink get its start?

The short story is that I ordered a cocktail at a Nashville bar ten years ago that absolutely blew my mind. It was called the Cannonball, and it featured rye whiskey and two amari. Until then, I had never tasted Averna or Meletti, much less heard of an amaro. So, I asked the bartender for his specs (which was very taboo at the time), he obliged, and then I bought every bottle the next day. Similar to how a home cook learns from recipes, I became obsessed with cocktail books. I pored over the classics (pun intended) and found new recipes to try. Or, I would hear a new & interesting bottle call my name from the liquor store, then find as many recipes with that ingredient as possible. When I learned what I liked and didn't like, my focus turned to making riffs on popular cocktails and then to creating new recipes altogether.

Now for the longer story . . .

Prior to launching Soundtrack My Drink as a full-time job, I spent fifteen years in marketing for retail and hospitality. I started as a graphic designer in 2007, but eventually ran music, entertainment, and social media for a large footwear company. And after jumping to hospitality during the pandemic, I steered partnerships for an international hotel chain. Marketing and storytelling have felt like second nature to me for a very long time.

Soundtrack My Drink started as a vanity project. Early on, it was a way to curb my creative burnout at work and to blend two of the worlds I love the most—music and cocktails. For a while, my little Instagram account was just a fun hobby. I connected with other creators, bartenders, and brands from all over the world. I found my voice and defined my taste. I learned as much as I could about cocktails and cocktail photography. I discovered new music. And, somewhere along the way, I realized there was untapped potential in what I was building.

I became more confident in my tastes, both in music and in cocktails. And I started to define a relationship between the two. Music, for example, is a really effective way to introduce someone to an unfamiliar ingredient or cocktail: "Hey, this song by your favorite band sounds even better when you're drinking a Negroni." Similarly, a cocktail can help introduce people to new music. Have you ever listened to old-school hip-hop while drinking an Old Fashioned? It'll blow your mind.

In December 2022, I turned my hobby into an LLC, and became a full-time consultant. I'm trying to push the boundaries of what my business can be—recipe development, content creation, agency-adjacent business development, private bartending, home bar concierge, playlist curation, etc.

Cheers to great drinks, great music, and to following your passion!

THE CORNER'S DILEMMA

SOUNDTRACK MY DRINK

Nashville has long been known for its music scene, but the city is also filled with great beer and whiskey. So, here's a riff from Adam Sloan, owner of Soundtrack My Drink, on a Whiskey Sour that combines both beer and whiskey. Because sometimes you shouldn't have to choose. Named after a song by Nashville punk rockers Free Throw, this recipe steals its sweetness from a house-made salted demerara syrup and cherry liqueur, and balances that sweetness with bitter notes from an unexpected splash of brewski.

GLASSWARE: Rocks glass

GARNISH: Skewered maraschino cherry

- 1½ oz. Nelson's Green Brier Tennessee Whiskey
- ½ oz. Heering Cherry Liqueur
- ¾ oz. fresh lemon juice
- ½ oz. Salted Demerara Syrup (see recipe)
- Splash pale ale beer

1. Fill your cocktail shaker halfway with ice then add all of the ingredients, except for the beer.

2. Shake for 10 to 15 seconds.

3. Add a splash of pale ale then double-strain the cocktail into a rocks glass over a large ice cube.

4. Garnish with a skewered maraschino cherry.

SALTED DEMERARA SYRUP: In a small saucepan, combine 2 cups hot water, and 2 large pinches coarse salt. Stir until dissolved, then add 2½ cups demerara sugar. Stir until the sugar has dissolved and let simmer on medium-low heat for 5 to 10 minutes, paying close attention not to let the mixture boil. Store refrigerated in an airtight container for up to 3 weeks.

STILL NOT A PLAYER

SOUNDTRACK MY DRINK

In the land of bachelorette parties, it's pretty much always 'pink drink szn' in Nashville," says Adam Sloan, owner of Soundtrack My Drink. "Rain or shine, but especially when it's hot. And speaking of hot weather, did you know that vinegar can help lower your body temperature? It's basically liquid air conditioning. For that reason, vinegar shrubs are the perfect hack for warm-weather cocktails. I love breaking up the monotony of Margaritas and Daiquiris by tossing in some vinegar. Or, we could get really crazy with an Improved Negroni cocktail like this one, inspired by the prophet Big Pun. I'm calling this pink drink Still Not a Player because . . . I can crush a lot of them."

GLASSWARE: **Rocks glass**

- 1½ oz. Hendrick's Gin
- 1 oz. Dolin Dry Vermouth
- ¾ oz. Blueberry Shrub (see recipe)
- ¼ oz. Luxardo Maraschino Originale
- Barspoon Absente Absinthe Refined
- 2 to 3 drops Saline Solution (see recipe)

1. Fill your cocktail shaker halfway with ice, then add all of the ingredients.

2. Shake for 10 to 15 seconds.

3. Double-strain the cocktail into a rocks glass over fresh ice.

SALINE SOLUTION: Add ¾ oz. coarse salt to 3 oz. hot water and stir until the salt is fully dissolved. Keep the solution in a dropper bottle.

BLUEBERRY SHRUB: Mix 1 cup white sugar and 1 cup blueberries together, mashing the blueberries to release the juices. Cover the mixture and leave it in the refrigerator for 48 hours. Stir it periodically. When everything is nice and mushy, add in 1 cup champagne vinegar (or white vinegar). Add secondary flavor agents (herbs or spices) if desired. Stir everything together and store the mixture in the refrigerator for up to 3 days. Do not agitate; let the vinegar bond with the fruit syrup. Remove any large fruit pieces, give everything one final stir, then double-strain the shrub into an airtight container. It will keep for 9 to 12 months in the refrigerator.

THUNDERBIRD

SOUNDTRACK MY DRINK

One of Adam Sloan's favorite flavor combinations is coffee and pineapple, which served as the inspiration for this slightly sweeter, smokier riff on a classic Jungle Bird. Named after a song from Hermanos Gutierrez, it pairs well with late nights and vinyl records.

GLASSWARE: Highball glass

GARNISH: Pineapple frond

- 1½ oz. Madre Mezcal Espadin
- ¾ oz. Heirloom Pineapple Amaro
- ½ oz. Amargo-Vallet Angostura
- ½ oz. Mr Black Cold Brew Coffee Liqueur
- ¼ oz. Burnt Honey Syrup (see recipe)
- 4 drops Saline Solution (see recipe on page 270)

1. In a mixing glass, combine all of the ingredients with ice and stir for 20 seconds.

2. Strain the cocktail into a highball glass over a Collins-style ice cube.

3. Garnish with a pineapple frond.

BURNT HONEY SYRUP: In a small saucepan over medium heat, add 2 cups honey. Bring it to a boil, stirring occasionally, and cook the honey until it darkens, about 2 to 3 minutes after the initial boil. Remove the pan from heat and slowly add 2 cups hot water. Stir until combined, then allow the syrup to cool. Store it in an airtight container for up to 2 to 3 weeks.

MAGIC STICK

Stirred vodka. Now that I have your attention," says Adam Sloan, "it's time to expand your mind, because stirred vodka isn't just for Martinis. Also, I really, really love the song 'Magic Stick' from the early 2000s. Personal opinion: Lil' Kim was one of the most underrated rappers from that time period, and 50 Cent was one of the most iconic—kinda like vodka and stirred cocktails."

GLASSWARE: Rocks glass

GARNISH: Cinnamon stick (optional)

- 1½ oz. Cinnamon-Infused Vodka (see recipe)
- ¾ oz. Cynar
- ½ oz. Giffard Banane du Brésil
- ½ oz. Centerbe Faccia Brutto
- Dash mole bitters
- 2 drops Saline Solution (see recipe on page 270)

1. Chill a rocks glass. In a mixing glass, combine all of the ingredients with ice and stir for 10 seconds.

2. Strain the cocktail into the chilled rocks glass with no ice.

3. If you prefer, garnish with a cinnamon stick.

CINNAMON-INFUSED VODKA: Crack 2 cinnamon sticks in half and drop them into a 750 ml bottle of Tito's Handmade Vodka. Seal the bottle and let it sit for 2 days. Strain before using.

THE GOLD RUSH

The Gold Rush is a beautifully simple, modern whiskey cocktail made with just three ingredients: bourbon, lemon juice, and honey syrup. This recipe's minimalistic approach allows flavors to shine through, with a harmonious balance between the rich, oaky bourbon, lemon's brightness, and the natural sweetness of honey. The result is a cocktail that is simultaneously refreshing, complex, and incredibly satisfying. Make a berry version by muddling fresh berries with the syrup before adding the remaining ingredients.

GLASSWARE: Double rocks glass
GARNISH: Lemon slice, edible flower

- **2 oz. bourbon**
- **¾ oz. fresh lemon juice**
- **¾ oz. Honey Syrup (see recipe)**

1. Add all of the ingredients to a shaker and fill it three-fourths of the way with ice.

2. Shake until chilled, then strain the cocktail into a double rocks glass filled with ice.

3. Garnish with a lemon slice and a seasonal edible flower.

HONEY SYRUP: In a container, combine 1 cup honey and ⅓ cup hot water and stir until the honey is dissolved.

EAST NASHVILLE

CHAMPURRADO OLD FASHIONED

KIMCHI BLOODY MARIA

UBE COLADA

MAYA BAY

MIDNIGHT ESPRESSO

STRAWBERRY CHEESECAKE SHAKE

STIRRA-CANE

LINK IN BIO

CELEBRATION OF FAILURE

FREQUENT FLYER

GREEN TOMATO MARGARITA

WALLFLOWER

DIRTY SALER

East Nashville, just across the Cumberland River from downtown, is a vibrant and eclectic neighborhood brimming with trendy shops, local restaurants, music venues, and great bars. The twenty-first century has seen East Nashville's pockets like bustling Five Points, Inglewood, Fatherland Street, and McFerrin Park all transform into a hub for the city's thriving music, restaurant, and bar scenes. In leafy Shelby Park, the Greenway is a paved tree-lined path winding along the Cumberland River. And of course, Nissan Stadium fills with crowds for Titans home games and whatever concert or event is on deck.

Here it feels distinctly different than the famous honky-tonk highway, and that's exactly why locals are grateful for East Nashville, especially on crowded weekends in Music City.

LAURA UNTERBERG,
THE FOX BAR & COCKTAIL CLUB

Sneak behind fast-casual Nicoletto's Italian spot for one of Nashville's very best cocktail destinations. The Fox Bar & Cocktail Club is East Nashville's cozy 1,000-square-foot bar that's prime for cocktail nerds with a wildly imaginative cocktail list, brilliant staff, and a deep roster of harder-to-find spirits in Music City.

The mixologists at The Fox are as much a part of the draw here as the plush, cozy 1920s Art Deco vibe. Here, all bartenders are encouraged to submit recipes, then the team workshops them to ensure each drink is a fit for the month's menu. As bar manager Laura Unterberg emphasizes, they like to start drinking trends rather than follow them, so the menus always offer something exciting for drinkers and non-booze drinkers alike.

Laura Unterberg has been with The Fox Bar & Cocktail Club since January 2020. Named StarChef's Rising Star of 2022, Laura is a certified executive bourbon steward and retail specialist for Angel's Envy Whiskey, with over a decade of bartending experience in New York, Virginia, and Tennessee. Her love of midcentury cocktails and heritage spirits brought her to The Fox, where she works to make the bar better and kinder each day. You can find Laura in Garden & Gun, Liquor.com, *Parade Magazine*, Punch.com, *Forbes,* and more.

What's your most memorable night behind the bar in your career?

My parents don't really drink, so I always enjoy the rare occasion when my family gets to see what I do for a living. It's equally exciting to see my co-workers' parents. Nothing beats a proud mom.

Most "Nashville" story you've experienced working at The Fox?

We've been visited by quite a few well-known musicians, and even in East Nashville we still see the pink cowboy hat–wearing crowds. But every day after the 2020 tornado, I went out with some of my co-workers to clear downed trees and houses. Ironically enough, wearing Jack Daniel's safety gloves I had from a cooperage tour years prior. It was peak Nashville, in the best imaginable way.

Where is your preferred bartenders' hang bar (besides your own spot)?

I'm a sucker for Rice Vice & Bastion.

What do you do in your spare time?

Still trying to find out what "spare time" is, hahaha. In between exe-cuting a new menu (and specials) each month at The Fox and working for a whiskey company, I enjoy antiquing and hosting friends.

What's your desert island drink of choice?

My desert island drink has got to be a Bamboo—stirred sherry and vermouth—hard to go wrong, and I could drink one every day and be happy. But on Broadway, you will see me unapologetically ordering Busch Lights and Vanilla Vodka-and-Diets. I'm not sure what a guilty pleasure is called if you don't feel guilty?

Preferred liquor/ingredient to play around with and why?

All of it. It's why we have 400+ bottles at The Fox; I truly love it all. But I do take special pride in highlighting forgotten and lesser-known single-origin spirits.

CHAMPURRADO OLD FASHIONED

THE FOX BAR & COCKTAIL CLUB
2905B GALLATIN PIKE

The Champurrado Old Fashioned has now been on our menu for several years now, and is a personal favorite," says Laura Unterberg. The Mole-Spiced Whiskey recipe yields 3 liters, and the Burnt Salted Honey recipe yields 2 quarts.

GLASSWARE: Double old-fashioned glass

GARNISH: Orange oil

- 1¾ oz. Mole-Spiced Whiskey (see recipe)
- ½ oz. mezcal
- ¼ oz. Paolucci Amaro CioCiaro
- ¼ oz. Burnt Salted Honey (see recipe)

1. Chill a double old-fashioned glass. In a mixing glass, combine all of the ingredients and fill the glass with ice, then stir.

2. Strain the cocktail over a large ice cube into the chilled double old-fashioned glass.

3. Garnish with a spray of orange oil.

BURNT SALTED HONEY: In a pan over low heat, combine 1 quart wildflower honey, 10 grams sea salt, and 1 quart water. Simmer, stirring frequently, until the mixture darkens in color. Remove from heat and let cool.

MOLE-SPICED WHISKEY: Heat the oven to 350°F. Spread 500 grams Cocoa Puffs in a thin layer on baking trays and lightly toast it in the oven. In a large container, whisk together 150 ml cold brew concentrate, ½ teaspoon ground cayenne pepper, and 2 teaspoons paprika to create a thin paste. Stir in 32 grams organic cacao nibs, 70 grams cracked cinnamon sticks, and the toasted cereal. Add 3 liters straight corn whiskey. Close the container and gently shake to incorporate the ingredients. Let the container rest at room temperature for 48 hours. Strain the mixture through a black-napkin–lined chinois, firmly squeezing the cereal to release the trapped liquid.

KIMCHI BLOODY MARIA

NOKO

701 PORTER ROAD

The classic Bloody Mary cocktail goes for an unexpected, unique twist thanks to bar manager Angel Lyle at Noko, Nashville's crowd-favorite, new-in-town, Asian-inspired, wood-fired restaurant. Noko's Kimchi Bloody Maria incorporates Asian staples such as fish sauce, kimchi, soy sauce, gochujang, and a shishito pepper garnish. The drink is also made with mezcal, which adds a smoky flavor that makes it the perfect pair with Asian-inspired dishes.

GLASSWARE: Highball glass
GARNISH: Fresh shishito pepper, charred

- **3 oz. Gochujang Bloody Maria Mix (see recipe)**
- **1½ oz. mezcal**
- **½ oz. fresh lemon juice**

1. Build the cocktail in a highball glass with ice and roll to finish.

2. Garnish with a charred shishito pepper.

GOCHUJANG BLOODY MARIA MIX: In a container of your choice, combine 3 oz. Charleston Bloody Mary Mix, ½ oz. kimchi liquid, 1¼ oz. fish sauce or soy sauce, 1 oz. lemon juice, and ¼ oz. gochujang.

UBE COLADA

NOKO
701 PORTER ROAD

At the wood-fired, Asian-inspired restaurant Noko, the Ube Colada is a vibrant tiki-inspired treat. Bacardí welcomes coconut, ube halaya (purple yam jam or spread), and pineapple for a true vacation from the swarming scooters and bachelorettes.

GLASSWARE: Large goblet or hurricane glass
GARNISH: Crumbled dehydrated fruit

- **2 oz. Don Papa Rum**
- **1 oz. coconut water**
- **1 oz. ube spread**
- **¾ oz. fresh pineapple juice**
- **½ oz. coconut milk**
- **Sweetened coconut cream, to top**

1. Add all of the ingredients, except for the cream, into a blender with a small scoop of ice and blend until smooth.

2. Pour the drink into a large goblet or hurricane glass.

3. Top with sweetened coconut cream.

4. Garnish with a crumbled, dehydrated fruit of your choice.

MAYA BAY

PEARL DIVER
1008 GALLATIN AVENUE

T his drink was a take-back of vacationing in Thailand and going to Maya Bay," says Jamie White. "It's not the easiest to source all the ingredients in Nashville. The process of finding everything we use at Pearl Diver is a fun one though. We get to spend a lot of time going to local international markets throughout the city and seeing what new and unique flavors have been imported here that we get to work with. The Maya Bay shows just that. This refreshing drink has a little bit of spice to it that makes it perfect to drink on a hot summer day and can transport you to the vacation life you might need!"

GLASSWARE: Highball glass

- **Mint, for the rim**
- **Red curry powder, for the rim**
- **Salt, for the rim**

- **2 oz. blanco tequila**
- **1½ oz. Mango Curry Mix (see recipe)**
- **¾ oz. fresh lime juice**

1. Wet the rim of a highball glass in water then dip the rim in equal parts mint, red curry powder, and salt.

2. Shake all of the remaining ingredients together in a cocktail shaker with ice.

3. Fine-strain the cocktail into the glass over ice.

MANGO CURRY MIX:
Add 1 cup mango purée, 6 oz. agave syrup (equal parts agave nectar and water), and 1 tablespoon red curry powder to a small saucepan and cook on medium until all of the ingredients are combined. Strain.

MIDNIGHT ESPRESSO

PEARL DIVER
1008 GALLATIN AVENUE

T he Espresso Martini has had the comeback of a lifetime since its creation in the 1980s," Jamie White says. "We all know Nashville is known to be a party town; there's not much of a better way to start off your night than with an espresso cocktail. At Pearl Diver, we use chai tea and vanilla as well as a rum base instead of vodka for a more rounded taste and mouthfeel." Pearl Diver uses coffee from Nashville-based Retrograde.

GLASSWARE: Nick & Nora glass
GARNISH: 3 espresso beans, coffee grounds, cinnamon

- 1¾ oz. Chai Vanilla Rum (see recipe)
- 1¼ oz. rested espresso
- ½ oz. Kahlúa

1. Chill a Nick & Nora glass. Shake all of the ingredients together in a cocktail shaker with ice.

2. Fine-strain the cocktail into the chilled Nick & Nora glass.

3. Garnish with espresso beans and a half-and-half dusting of coffee grounds and cinnamon.

CHAI VANILLA RUM: In a large container of your choice, combine 1 bottle of Flor de Caña 4 Extra Seco Rum, 6 chai tea bags, and ¼ cup vanilla syrup. Let the mixture steep at room temperature for 15 minutes.

STRAWBERRY CHEESECAKE SHAKE

THE PHARMACY BURGER PARLOR & BEER GARDEN
731 MCFERRIN AVENUE

A boozy milkshake on a summer afternoon in Nashville on the patio—that's one way to beat the heat (and a great excuse to day-drink). A velvety smooth combo of ice cream, house-made strawberry syrup, and fruit-forward rosé topped with white chocolate shavings is perfectly acceptable for dessert—or as a meal all its own.

GLASSWARE: Fountain glass

GARNISH: Strawberry, white chocolate flakes

- 3 scoops vanilla ice cream
- Rosé, as needed
- 1 oz. strawberry syrup

1. Scoop out three scoops of ice cream into a shaker tin.

2. Add rosé up to the second ice cream scoop.

3. Add the strawberry syrup.

4. Using a blender or food processor, blend the ingredients together.

5. Pour the shake into a fountain glass and garnish with a strawberry and white chocolate flakes.

BEAU GAULTIER, BAY 6

1101 MCKENNIE AVENUE SUITE 6

Don't judge a book by its cover, or, in this case, don't judge the quality of a bar by the fact that it's located in a former car wash. Ask just about any bartender in town what their go-to bar is, Bar 6 is probably the answer. It's Nashville's smallest, perhaps most unassuming bar, tucked into the sixth suite of contemporary "food court" The Wash in East Nashville. A true neighborhood hang with just fourteen indoor seats and 350 square feet of space, Bay 6 opened in 2022, but it already has its own unique identity within Nashville's bar scene. Bay 6 has something for everyone, with a list of cocktails on draft for those just passing through for a fast-casual experience alongside hand-built offerings using ingredients not often seen on a Nashville drink menu. Here is Beau Gaultier, operating partner and beverage director of Bay 6, in his own words.

"I've always been fascinated by food," Beau says. "Growing up, I remember spending hours watching reruns of Justin Wilson and *Emeril Live* (both culinary royalty in Louisiana) and mixing drinks for my uncles during football games and family gatherings. When I was 15, I started working in a po-boy shop tucked in the back of a gas station, and when I was 19, I started bartending at a steak house while in college. I continued bartending because I got an English degree."

"Joking aside, I've been in the industry for over a decade now and have become absolutely smitten with the reality that I put drinks in cups, tell stories, and hang out for a living. I moved to Nashville about five years ago for funsies, honestly . . . I knew I was ready to move out of Baton Rouge, and knew I wasn't good enough at saying no to move to New Orleans. For me, Nashville was (and is) a great balance of city living and Southern kindness."

What has been your most memorable night behind the bar? Any fun Nashville stories or moments?

I've had more "don't meet your heroes" moments than I'd prefer to admit, and even more moments where I've made an ass out of myself. Here's one: when I was younger, I was told I looked like (and could be mistaken for) Sam Palladio (Gunnar Scott from the show *Nashville*). One night, when I was just a touch too drunk, I saw him at East Side Bowl, walked up to him and said, "People say I look like you." He said, very handsomely and Australian-ly, "I don't see it."

What's your "bartenders' hang" bar of choice?

Wilburn Street Tavern is the ultimate bartender's bar. It's got a deceptively impressive spirits selection, great bar snacks, and the perfect number of dark corners to hide from the public in.

Can you send a few of your perfect Nashville bar playlist recommendations?

My Bay 6 playlist (Beau 6 on Spotify) is my personal favorite. It's a mix of 2000s pop punk and West Coast rap—essentially a Tony Hawk knockoff playlist.

What's your recommended at-home bar tools/ingredients to have on hand?

My favorite home bar ingredient is food grade lemon and orange oil that I store in perfume atomizers and use in place of fresh citrus peels. You'll never need zest for your Old Fashioned or freezer Martini again.

Favorite spirit/ingredient to play around with when you're not working?

I love playing with flavored seltzers at the house—you can add a TON of flavor to really simple cocktails without worrying about affecting sweetness (or having any fancy cordials/infusions at the house).

What are the best and worst things about the bachelorette parties that the "new Nashville" is known for?

In this industry, it's really easy to get jaded about your job. It's easy to forget just how cool the job is and that the experience you're creating is really special. Seeing people come from different cities, and just being *excited* about everything is always really infectious to me. That said, the worst thing about bachelorette parties? Separate checks. If you're wanting to be a better tourist, close out on one card and split it with a check-splitting app. Even better, put it on *your* card and reap the credit card rewards points.

What is your go-to cocktail of choice?

A Suntory Highball is an absolute all-timer for me. It's like tortilla chips at a Tex-Mex restaurant: I'll order one while I figure out what I *really* want. But if I'm feeling fancy? Not much beats a well-made French 75 for me.

STIRRA-CANE

BAY 6
1101 MCKENNIE AVENUE SUITE 6

This cocktail, a New Orleans Hurricane dressed up in a suit, comes from the Hurricane Season menu at Bay 6, a tongue-in-cheek late summer menu that focused on classic New Orleans cocktails, according to Beau Gaultier. It uses a blend of aged and unaged rums with blackstrap bitters to avoid the cloying sweetness of a traditional blackstrap rum, a splash of passion fruit liqueur for some tropical flair, and a lime coin (the sliced "cheek" of a lime that includes a bit of zest and a bit of the flesh of the fruit) for flavor and a touch of acidity to create a stirred, boozy sipper with all the flavor of the traditional party crusher.

GLASSWARE: Coupe or martini glass

GARNISH: Lime peel

- 1 oz. aged rum
- 1 oz. unaged rum
- ¼ oz. Giffard Crème de Fruits de la Passion
- 1 lime coin
- Dash Bittercube Blackstrap Bitters

1. Chill a coupe or martini glass. Add all of the ingredients to a mixing glass.

2. Stir with ice for 20 seconds.

3. Strain the cocktail into the chilled coupe or martini glass.

4. Garnish with a lime peel.

LINK IN BIO

BAY 6
1101 MCKENNIE AVENUE SUITE 6

E very version of the Bay 6 menu has some version of this cocktail on it (a low-proof sherry-based patio crusher)," says Beau Gaultier. "It's become one of my favorite slots to fill on the menu and is a fantastic way to introduce guests to sherry's utility in a cocktail bar." Beau advises home mixologists to be selective with the passion fruit liqueur you choose for this recipe, as some (like Chinola and Passoã) will affect the overall acidity of the cocktail.

GLASSWARE: Collins glass

GARNISH: Mint bouquet, grapefruit slice

- 1½ oz. fino sherry
- ½ oz. Marie Brizard White Cocoa Liqueur
- ½ oz. Giffard Crème de Fruits de la Passion
- ¾ oz. fresh lemon juice
- ¼ oz. simple syrup
- Champagne, to top

1. Add all of the ingredients, except for the Champagne, to a cocktail shaker and shake with ice.

2. Strain the cocktail into a collins glass filled with ice.

3. Top with Champagne.

4. Garnish with a mint bouquet and grapefruit slice.

CELEBRATION OF FAILURE

BAY 6
1101 MCKENNIE AVENUE SUITE 6

In this savory riff on a Sherry Collins, jammy Madeira gets juiced up with stone fruit, sage, and wheat beer, along with a naughty dash of tamari (a low-gluten soy sauce) for salinity and complexity. "When I start collecting submissions for the fall cocktail menu, I have one rule: no baking spices," says Beau Gaultier. "This forces the team at Bay 6 to make some cocktails that feel like fall without falling (haha) into the same old tricks."

GLASSWARE: Collins glass

GARNISH: Orange slice

- ½ oz. simple syrup
- 5 sage leaves
- 1½ oz. Madeira
- ¾ oz. fresh lemon juice
- 13 drops tamari
- ½ oz. Giffard Abricot du Roussillon
- Hefeweizen or wheat beer, to top

1. Add the simple syrup and sage leaves to a cocktail shaker and muddle gently.

2. Add the remaining ingredients, except for the beer, and shake with ice.

3. Fine-strain the cocktail into a collins glass filled with ice.

4. Top with wheat beer and garnish with an orange slice.

FREQUENT FLYER

T his cocktail is made as a sort of cheeky version of an Espresso Martini," says Beau Gaultier, operating partner and beverage director of Bay 6. "It uses high corn-content bourbon to balance out espresso liqueur, a homemade miso syrup, cream, and a full egg. What results is a creamy, sweet-and-salty flip that's perfect for converting Espresso Martini fanatics into whiskey drinkers and whiskey nerds into Espresso Martini lovers."

GLASSWARE: Coupe or martini glass

GARNISH: Grated espresso beans

- 1½ oz. Mellow Corn Straight Corn Whiskey
- ½ oz. Caffè Borghetti
- ½ oz. Miso Syrup (see recipe)
- ½ oz. cream
- 1 egg

1. Chill a coupe or martini glass. Add all of the ingredients to a shaker tin.

2. Shake without ice for roughly 5 seconds.

3. Add ice and shake for 10 seconds.

4. Strain the cocktail into the chilled coupe or martini glass and garnish with grated espresso beans.

MISO SYRUP: Combine 50 grams miso and 500 grams simple syrup in a small pot. Bring the mixture to simmer, stirring to incorporate. Strain the syrup before using.

ERIC JEFFUS, AUDREY AND JUNE

809 MERIDIAN STREET

Originally hailing from Southern California, Eric Jeffus is currently the bar director at Audrey and June, two of Sean Brock's dining concepts in Nashville that explore Southern and Appalachian cuisine.

A veteran in the restaurant industry, Eric made the switch to bartending in 2010, followed by a move to New York, where, in the world of fine dining and craft cocktails, and found that bartending is just like a well-balanced cocktail—equal parts alchemy, theatricality, and counseling. He bartended at a Michelin-starred French restaurant, Café Boulud, for three years before heading to Chicago to work under chef Grant Achatz of Alinea as a bartender at The Aviary, then The Office, the speakeasy underneath The Aviary centered around dealer's choice cocktails.

In 2023, Eric transitioned into his role at Audrey and June and took up residence in East Nashville, which is central to the people, bars, and restaurants that inspire him. When he is not crafting experiences for guests at Audrey or June, you can find him reading, enjoying drinks, or playing Magic: The Gathering.

What did you want to be when you grew up?

I wanted to be a toy designer when I was a kid—clearly a desire to spark joy in people is deeply ingrained in me. I went to school to be a professor of English, and I still think of myself as an educator, just with a much more dynamic classroom. Studying and understanding the world, and finding the best way to share that with others, is still my goal.

What brought you to Nashville?

I came to Nashville because of a dear, longtime friend who grew up in Carthage, now living with her husband in Mt. Juliet, who coaxed me down from Chicago a few years ago when I was looking to move. She told me a burgeoning bar and restaurant scene was developing here, and she was dead right.

What drew you to this restaurant/bar?

Most of my bartending experience is from fine dining restaurants, cultures driven by the vision of forward-thinking chefs, and when I learned that The Continental was paying homage to the old-world fine dining I've come to love, and that friends from my past and present were already working there, I could hardly resist. I stayed at Continental for the better part of a year before June opened, and then I moved over to help cultivate the tasting menu environment there.

In general, though, I'm drawn to our company's focus on flavor and ingredients, on exploring what's possible and synthesizing tradition and modern ideology. I learn quickly and get bored easily, so I appreciate an ever-moving target.

What's your go-to cocktail order?

I'm a simple man at the end of the day. I don't have just one "go-to" cocktail, but I tend to prefer classics. I'll never refuse a well-made Daiquiri, Old Fashioned, or Manhattan.

What is your favorite bartenders' hang bar?

I feel like most of the places where I hang out are popular among bartenders, but I spend the most time at Lakeside Lounge, a neighborhood dive bar owned by the folks from Attaboy. I'm also a big fan of Martha My Dear and Bay 6 (in The Wash), which make absolutely fantastic cocktails and provide great service.

What are must-have things to have on hand for someone's bar at home?

The first thing I tell home bartenders is that CARING is the first tool in their arsenal. If you don't care, you can't make truly good drinks. What do I mean by "caring"? I mean paying attention to, studying, questioning, analyzing, celebrating, investing in. If you want to learn more, that's the first big step in your journey.

Outside of that, you'll just need something to measure with. If you're making a batch for friends, measuring cups work great. For one drink (and for style points), it's worth picking up a good set of jiggers. As for other "bar tools," anyone who tells you that you need shaker tins and mixing glasses to make a drink is trying to sell you something. Mason jars (or, really, anything with a lid) to shake, and rocks glasses to stir. Everything else is just for flair.

I love your attention to zero-proof pairings with the tasting menu at June. What is your process like for creating these pairings? What's your favorite booze-free drink you've made?

Thank you so much! It's been truly exciting to explore what can be accomplished in terms of zero-proof pairings with enough attention, and I'm humbled that other people are noticing.

As for my process, it's just a bit chaotic but it works. About two weeks from the launch of a new menu, I'll learn the flavors of each dish, course by course. A lot of what I do initially is what I call "composing in my head," or building a mental flavor association map to think about pairings. What are the flavors that anchor each dish in the memory, and what ingredients will either complement or contrast those flavors and tie them together to provide a noteworthy pairing? I use a variety of culinary and scientific disciplines and resources and consult many of the talented minds and palates I work with on a daily basis, before settling on a final recipe.

One of my favorite zero-proof pairings recently was designed to pair with a savory-sweet blue cheese cheesecake with pickled pear, fennel marmalade, and fig leaves. My pairing was a combination of Milky Oolong from High Garden with the liquid from "pear-boshi" (pears that were salt-pickled in the Lab in the manner of Japanese umeboshi), and a kombucha made in the Lab from honeysuckle black tea. A simple combination of ingredients, but quite complex.

The NA scene is, excitingly, finally growing here in town. What is most exciting to you about this as a beverage director? I know a lot of people really hate when I order a drink sans booze. What makes you see this differently?

What matters most to me is flavor, not booze. I've been a bartender for a long time now, and alcohol is a very useful medium for flavor, but it's not my raison d'être—flavor is. As such, I'm all for better zero-proof options, as flavor finally has a chance to catch up in that arena. I find it deeply gratifying that I have a chance to create thoughtful, commensurate beverages for people who aren't drinking (for whatever reason, doesn't matter to me), and they get to experience something they may have given up on — a complex and curated beverage option.

I feel like a bartender growing angry at a zero-proof order has a limited viewpoint, but it's not necessarily their fault. If they work at a place where NA options haven't been considered, it's frustrating to cobble together some sort of "fancy lemonade" for guests seeking an option without alcohol, as they don't have resources to improve much upon that bleak prospect. If they're concerned about check averages, then it would help them to know that, if you create a thoughtful beverage using nonalcoholic spirits (which aren't cheap), you can demand a price commensurate with the quality of the product.

As the saying goes, "If you build it, they will come."

GREEN TOMATO MARGARITA

AUDREY/JUNE
809 MERIDIAN STREET

Y ou say, "tomato," Eric Jeffus says, "cocktail time." The bar director for both of Sean Brock's flagship restaurants, Audrey and June, makes sure each drink pairs well with food, but also stands on its own with interesting, hyperlocal ingredients and eloquence.

GLASSWARE: Rocks glass
GARNISH: Freshly ground white pepper

- 1 oz. Don Fulano Blanco Tequila
- ¾ oz. Salted Green Tomato Juice (see recipe)
- ¾ oz. Green Peppercorn Syrup (see recipe)
- ½ oz. Banhez Mezcal
- ½ oz. fresh lime juice

1. Combine all of the ingredients with ice in a shaker tin and shake vigorously.

2. Strain the cocktail into a rocks glass, add fresh ice, and garnish with fresh white pepper from a pepper grinder.

SALTED GREEN TOMATO JUICE: Chop green tomatoes into quarters and put them through a Breville juicer, then fine-strain the juice to refine the texture. Add 4 teaspoons 20% Saline Solution (see recipe) for every 16 oz. of strained green tomato juice.

GREEN PEPPERCORN SYRUP: Combine 3 cups white sugar, 3 cups water, 2 tablespoons green peppercorns, and 1 tablespoon white peppercorns in a saucepan and bring the mixture to a boil. Turn down the heat and simmer the mixture 15 to 20 minutes, then blend it in a blender (crank it for at least a couple minutes), then fine-strain the syrup to remove fine particles using a "superbag," also known as a "nut milk bag."

20% SALINE SOLUTION: Combine 80 grams warm water and 20 grams high-quality salt and mix thoroughly until the salt dissolves. This is the highest concentration of salt that water can hold, so it's possible some particulate will remain. Strain off the excess salt or ignore it.

JORDAN SPAULDING, FOLK

823 MERIDIAN STREET

Jordan Spaulding, bar manager at one of Nashville's best restaurants, Folk, started bartending ten years ago. Now you can find him behind the bar running the beverage program at Folk in East Nashville full-time, while focusing new efforts on his cocktail pop-up, Haven (@haven_nsh), around the country.

What led you on your career path and your move to Nashville?

Back in 2012, I moved to Boston to attend college for physics, with the goal of teaching. My first mentor and boss at the time, Sarah Hanson, showed me the academic side of alcohol and how incredible it can be to have a rotating attendance of "students" every day, with different curiosities, at the bar. From there I was hooked and dove into beverage education in any aspect I could. Flash forward to 2020 and with the pandemic setting in, it was time to find a new city to call home. I had visited Nashville a few times prior and always loved the burgeoning food and beverage scene here and that people here were excited to try anything. Makes for a fun place to embrace creativity.

To be a standout in both food and beverage is a testament to the work you do at Folk. How do you make both zero-proof and regular drinks shine at a place that draws crowds in for the food?

Approachability is key. In a world with such an ease of access to every technique and all the equipment, it's important that a drink should still be relatable. Using savory flavors to tie in a basic understanding and descriptors that paint a scene or a feeling that the drink encapsulates helps make guests feel comfortable sorting through unknown ingredients.

When you're off work, where will we find you having a drink?

If I'm staying local, its Wilburn Street Tavern for the solid beer-and-a-shot special and walkability. Plus, it's rarely crowded, and I love a good patio. If I've got a day off? You can usually find me sneaking off to Attaboy at least once a week for a Martini.

What's your go-to drink order?

Fords Gin Officers' Reserve 50/50 Martini. Stirred. Garnished with a lemon twist.

Favorite spirit/ingredient to play with and why?

Sherry! I love fortified wines, but sherry specifically encapsulates an extreme level of finesse in distillation, combined with a historic methodology for aging, and it has flavors and textures not found in any other product on the planet. Such a variance in styles creates something to grab for use in any season as well.

WALLFLOWER

I wanted to utilize ingredients from areas that had historically been overlooked from a beverage perspective," says Jordan Spaulding. "Appalachian-inspired Southern amaro, Sicilian amaro, and a savory punched Swedish aquavit make for a wildly herbaceous but curious sipping cocktail."

GLASSWARE: Nick & Nora glass

- 1¼ oz. High Wire Distilling Southern Amaro Liqueur
- 1¼ oz. Amaro Averna
- ¾ oz. O.P. Anderson Original Aquavit

1. In a mixing glass, lightly stir all of the ingredients together with ice.

2. Strain the cocktail into any stemmed glass (preferably a Nick & Nora).

DIRTY SALER

I 've always found dirty Martinis to be unpredictable and often aggressively well, filthy," says Jordan Spaulding. "This was my back-pocket answer to meet in the middle of the Martini world, creating a salty, seeded, savory note upfront that slowly shifts to a botanical, vegetal profile with a long, dry finish."

GLASSWARE: Coupe glass

GARNISH: Olive and orange peel on a skewer

- 1¼ oz. Plymouth Gin
- 1¼ oz. O.P. Anderson Original Aquavit
- ¼ oz. Salers Gentian Aperitif
- ¼ oz. Castelvetrano olive brine
- 2 dashes orange bitters

1. Combine all of the ingredients in a mixing glass with ice.

2. Stir until the mixture is ice cold.

3. Strain the cocktail into a coupe.

4. Garnish with an orange peel and an olive on a skewer.

ACKNOWLEDGMENTS

I am so incredibly grateful to my small but mighty circle of family and friends who have loved, supported, and encouraged me throughout the journey of creating my first book alongside navigating the grief journey of losing two parents. I'd like to dedicate this book to my two amazing sets of parents. To my Mama and Fred, on the other side, thank you for your generosity, unending love, and for always being my biggest cheerleaders. I miss you but carry you with me in all I do. To Dad and Carolyn, thank you for your continued support, love, and friendship during the toughest years of my life. I'm so grateful to have you both.

To the brilliant bartenders of Nashville, past and present, thank you so much for sharing your talents with locals, millions of tourists, and myself regularly. Cheers, y'all; I hope people tip you well and remind you daily that you are a huge part of the symphony that makes Music City the worldwide tourist destination it is today. This project would not have been possible without your contributions, passion, and assistance.

Nashville, I'm so grateful I have such an incredible place to call home, when all sense of home has felt lost.

—Delia Jo

ABOUT THE AUTHOR

Delia Jo Ramsey writes about all things food-, drink-, and travel-related in Nashville. You can follow her on Instagram at @diningwithdeliajo and find her work at diningwithdeliajo.com.

PHOTO CREDITS

Page 55 Mayter Scott; 100, 103 Sean McGee; 111, 112, 115, 116, 119, 121, 122, 125 Camille Tambunting; 148–149 Heather Durham; 152 Sam Calderon; 228, 231, 233, 260 Phillip Fryman; 317 Sam Angel.

Pages 9, 10–11 courtesy of Library of Congress.

1, 3, 4–5, 6, 13, 15, 16, 17, 22–23, 31, 44–45, 67, 68–69, 104–105, 128–129, 142–143, 165, 175, 176–177, 197, 198–199, 207, 211, 212, 220–221, 222–223, 234–235, 258–259, 277, 278–279 used under official license from Shutterstock.com.

Page 91 by Pylyp Sukhenko on Unsplash.

All other images courtesy of the respective bars, restaurants, and profile subjects.

INDEX

—ABOUT CIDER MILL PRESS BOOK PUBLISHERS—

Good ideas ripen with time. From seed to harvest, Cider Mill Press brings fine reading, information, and entertainment together between the covers of its creatively crafted books. Our Cider Mill bears fruit twice a year, publishing a new crop of titles each spring and fall.

"Where Good Books Are Ready for Press"
501 Nelson Place
Nashville, Tennessee 37214
cidermillpress.com